York Minster

FRONT COVER: *The majestic west front of York Minster, seen from Museum Street.*
BACK COVER: *An aerial view showing the Minster dwarfing the church of St Michael-le-Belfrey, reconstructed in 1525–37, where Guy Fawkes was baptized in 1570.*
TOP: *The Minster from the south-west, dominating the rooftops of the ancient city.*

ABOVE: *This finely carved stone boss depicting the Assumption of the Blessed Virgin Mary is in the vaulting of the entrance arch of the choir screen.*

YORK MINSTER

Reginald Cant, Canon Emeritus of York Minster

A 'minster' was a missionary centre in the early days of Christianity in Anglo-Saxon England. The word comes from the Latin *monasterium* which could describe any church served by a group of clergy. York Minster was never a monastic church, but from the beginning of its history was a cathedral, because it was the headquarters of a bishop, and contained his *cathedra*, the chair in which he sat and which represented his authority to teach, to govern and to lead the worship. Today the Minster's official description is 'the cathedral and metropolitical church of St Peter in York'. It means that the Minster is the chief church of the northern province of the Church of England, as well as of the diocese of York, and is the seat of an archbishop. Here take place the consecration of newly appointed Anglican bishops for the north, the ordination of clergy for service in the diocese, many great diocesan and provincial gatherings, and an increasing number of united ecumenical services, as well as the daily round of worship – Matins, Holy Communion and Evensong – according to the Anglican tradition. It has been a house of prayer for hundreds of years, and now, newly restored and cleaned, it welcomes within its doors nearly two million visitors each year, of all races and creeds, and conveys to them, through its great beauty, some sense of the spiritual dimension of human life.

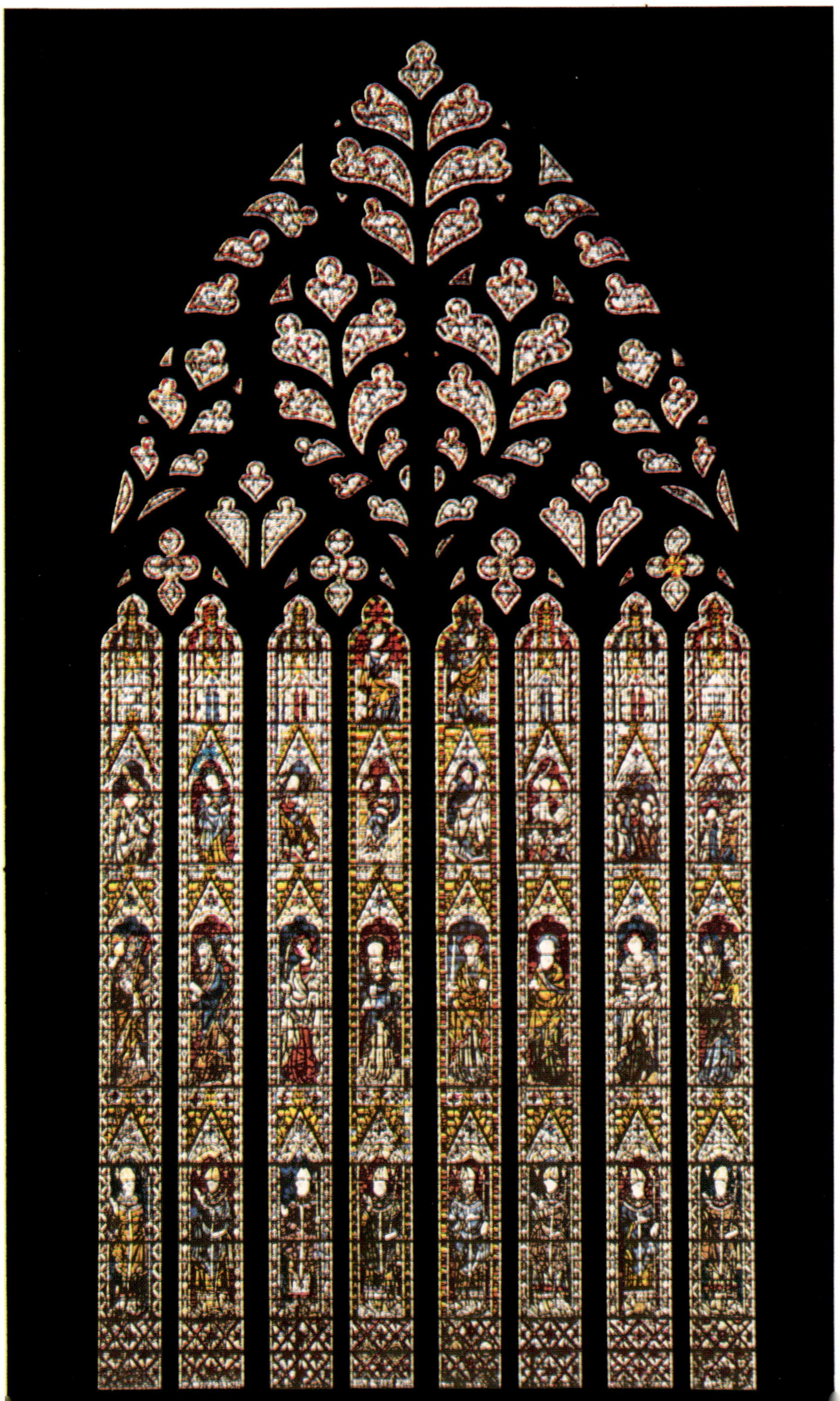

Early History

York, under the name Eboracum, was a Roman military centre of the greatest importance, and evidence of the size and splendour of its buildings may be seen in the Undercroft museum which has been constructed amid the massive new concrete and steel foundations of the 1970s. It is entered from the south transept and is fully described at the end of this book. Under the present south transept lay part of the headquarters of the legionary fortress. It housed the sixth legion of 5,600 highly trained heavy infantry and from it the province of *Britannia Inferior* was administered.

It was in Roman York that there occurred an event which was to be followed by consequences momentous for the history of the world. In A.D. 306 Constantius, ruler of the west, died among his troops in York, and they forthwith acclaimed his son Constantine as Caesar. At the time the empire

Continued on page 8

★

LEFT: *The great west window was given by Archbishop William Melton in 1338. The stonework of the tracery suggests the shape of a heart. The top row of glass panels has New Testament scenes, the second the apostles, and the third a series of archbishops.*

FACING PAGE: *The nave, looking east. The pulpit was designed by Sir Ninian Comper in 1948. The brass eagle lectern dates from 1686.*

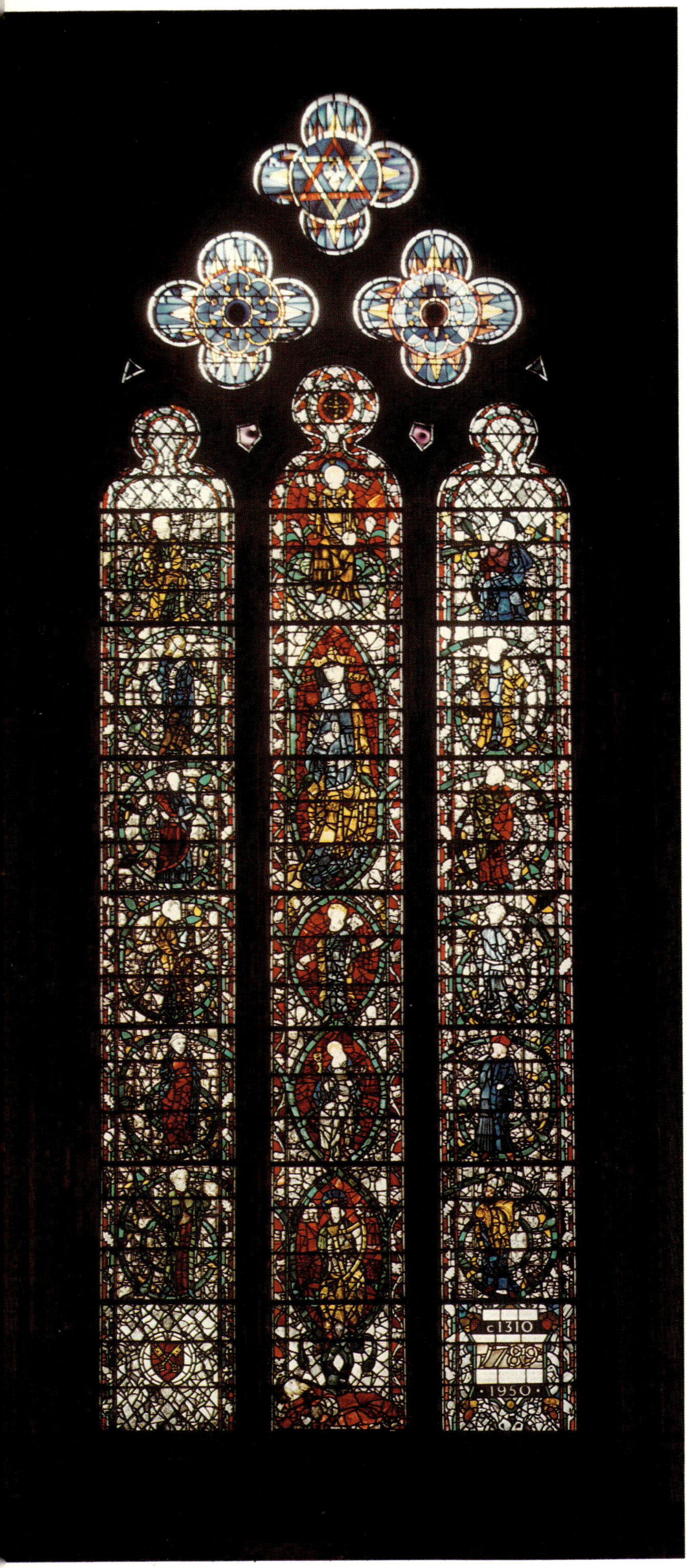

FACING PAGE, LEFT: *The 14th-century Jesse Stem window. Reading from bottom to top, the figures are (left) Elisha, Habakkuk, Ezekiel, Isaiah, Daniel and Moses; (centre) Jesse, David, Solomon, Josiah, The Virgin Mary and Christ; (right) Hosea, Joel, Malachi, Ezra, Samuel and Elijah.*

FACING PAGE, ABOVE RIGHT: *The window at the south-west end of the nave (1338). Two Roman soldiers guard the crucified Christ, while the donor, Thomas de Beneston, kneels at the foot, with Our Lady on the left and St John on the right.*

FACING PAGE, BELOW RIGHT: *The 12th-century St Nicholas panel, over the entrance to the shop, depicts the legend of a posthumous miracle by the saint. A Jewish money-lender, having been cheated by a Christian, called upon St Nicholas to intercede. Swift retribution fell upon the cheat, who was run over by a horse-drawn cart. The Jew was so impressed that he was converted to Christianity.*

ABOVE: *The choir screen, built 1475–1500, is adorned with statues of kings of England from William the Conqueror to Henry VI. All are contemporary with the screen, except that on the extreme right, which dates from 1810. The stucco angels were also added in the 19th century. The figure of Christ over the entrance is modern.*

RIGHT: *The tomb of Archbishop Walter de Gray (d. 1225), who began the building of the present Minster.*

was not under unified control, but within a few years he had become sole emperor and in his march to power had assumed the role of protector of the Church. With him began the alliance of Church and State which was to form the inspiration of the Christian civilization of the Middle Ages. Nothing is known of Christianity in Roman York save the name of Bishop Eborius who attended the council of Arles in 314. The Roman soldiers withdrew about 380, and there is a long blank in the record until the establishment of the Anglo-Saxon Northumbrian kingdom three centuries later, but the archaeological evidence suggests that the buildings continued to be used

On Easter Eve, 627, the Northumbrian king Edwin accepted Christianity and was baptized in a small, square wooden oratory built for the occasion. It is not known where this was. It could have been in the courtyard of the *principia* beneath the present south transept. He had been moved to take this step by his wife, a Christian princess from Kent named Ethelburga, by his own experiences a year or two earlier when he was in exile in East Anglia, and by the persuasion of the bishop Paulinus who had been sent from Rome as a missionary by Pope Gregory the Great and had accompanied the princess from Canterbury. Pope Gregory the Great had planned that York should be the northern ecclesiastical capital, and the dedication of the Minster in the name of St Peter is a sign of its early association with Rome.

The historian Bede tells a story which hints at the deeper reasons which may have led Edwin to accept the new faith. He tells of the advice given to the king by one of his counsellors. He compared the life of man with the flight of a lone sparrow through the banqueting hall where in the winter months the king sat with his thanes. Inside was warmth and light, which the bird enjoyed for a brief moment before it flew out again into the winter storms, back to the darkness from which it came. Man, too, was ignorant of what went before and what followed this life, and if the new teaching could give more certain knowledge then it should be followed.

A stone church soon replaced the first minster. Because of political troubles it fell into disrepair. It was renovated by St Wilfrid in 670, and finally perished during the Norman Conquest. Northumbrian Christianity was a blend of two missionary movements: one inspired by Pope Gregory of Rome and the other from Ireland via Iona and the north. The union of the Roman and Celtic traditions was fittingly symbolized in the consecration of Cuthbert of Lindisfarne as bishop by Theodore of Tarsus in York Minster in the year 685. The most illustrious name connected with York during these centuries was that of Alcuin (*c*.735–804), head of the York cathedral school, who migrated to the Continent and became one of the emperor Charlemagne's chief advisers and a leader in the contemporary revival of learning. In his day the library of York Minster was famous in western Europe. No tangible remains of the church of his day have so far been discovered.

Recent excavations have, however, revealed the plan of the Norman minster begun in 1070 by the first Norman archbishop, Thomas of Bayeux. For further information readers are recommended to consult *A History of York Minster*, edited by G. E. Aylmer and R. Cant (Oxford, 1977) and *Excavations at York Minster, II: The Cathedral of Archbishop Thomas of Bayeux, York*, by Derek Phillips (HMSO, London, 1985). Thomas helped to formulate a new system of government for the secular (i.e. non-monastic) cathedrals which still provides the basis of the division of duties between their officials – the dean, precentor, chancellor and treasurer. His new church, deliberately built on an east-west axis across the south-east/north-west alignment of the Roman fortress (which had been followed by later Saxon burials in the area) must have been one of the largest stone buildings

north of the Alps in the eleventh century. Part of its eastern foundations may be seen through a trap-door in the eastern crypt, and more may be learnt of it by a visit to the Undercroft. Archbishop Roger of Pont L'Evêque (1154–81), a colleague and critic of Thomas Becket, rebuilt the choir, and remains of it may be seen in the western crypt.

This building was the cathedral of York until the present Minster was built. It was the cathedral of York's saint, William Fitzherbert, whose remains now rest in the western crypt. William Fitzherbert, son of Herbert, Chamberlain to Henry I, and Emma, half sister of King Stephen (but not herself of royal blood), was treasurer of York Minster and archdeacon of the East Riding at the time of the retirement of Thurstan, archbishop 1119–40. He was appointed archbishop in 1143 after a tangled dispute as to Thirstan's successor. The dissenting canons protested to Rome and to the influential Bernard (later St Bernard), Abbot of Clairvaux, the Cistercian monastery in Champagne. They alleged undue influence by William's uncle, Henry of Blois, Bishop of Winchester, referred to by Bernard of Clairvaux as 'the whore of Winchester'. Nothing came of this protest immediately, but when Pope Lucius II died he was succeeded by Pope Eugenius III, a disciple of Bernard. In 1147 he deposed William Fitzherbert, appointing Henry Murdac in his place. In 1153, the year in which the Pope, Henry Murdac and Bernard of Clairvaux all died, William Fitzherbert was restored as archbishop. He returned to York in triumph in 1154 and it is said that such a vast crowd gathered on the bridge over the Ouse to welcome him that it collapsed, and yet no one was injured or drowned. This was attributed to William's prayers. Certainly there is much evidence of the love and

★

FACING PAGE: *The central tower. The present lantern tower replaces a bell-tower which collapsed in 1407. It is in the Perpendicular style, planned by Henry IV's master mason, William of Colchester, and finished in 1480. In 1966–7 it was discovered that the four piers were sinking unevenly and restoration work was begun. Visitors to the Undercroft will see the modern concrete and steel which now reinforce the foundations.*

ABOVE RIGHT: *The choir, looking east. On the left is the pulpit and on the right the Archbishop's throne.*

RIGHT: *The choir stalls were built after the fire of 1829, and are an exact replica of the earlier ones.*

reverence of local people towards him. On his return, William made peace with the Cistercians of Fountains Abbey and showed a desire to be on good terms with his former enemies. However, on 8 June 1154, he was taken ill and died soon after celebrating Solemn Mass. Archdeacon Osbert was suspected of having administered poison and was defrocked and forced to resign.

In the Middle Ages an important factor in bringing pilgrims, and therefore income, to a cathedral was the possession of a local saint. Perhaps as a counter to St John of Beverley and St Wilfrid of Ripon, much campaigning by the Chapter in the early 1200s led to the canonization of St William of York in 1227. In 1284 his remains were transferred from the nave to a new shrine behind the high altar, which soon became a place of veneration and pilgrimage, where miraculous cures were said to have happened. The shrine was destroyed at the time of the Reformation and St William's remains reinterred in the nave. (Parts of the shrine can be seen in the Yorkshire Museum.) During the work on the foundations between 1967 and 1972 St William's remains had to be disturbed and the Dean and Chapter resolved to move them to the western part of the crypt and to set up a small chapel there for ecumenical use. Not infrequently permission is granted to groups of Roman Catholics to hold private masses with their own priests at the shrine of St William.

It was in the twelfth-century choir of the Norman church that the wedding of Edward III and Philippa of Hainault was celebrated in 1328. Their son, Prince William, died as a child and his effigy is in the north choir aisle of the present building.

Norman archbishops often resisted the claims of the see of Canterbury to precedence, and the dispute was not settled until the fourteenth century. It was then that the present titles of the two archbishops were defined by Pope Innocent VI: York was to be Primate of England, but Canterbury to be Primate of *all* England.

There are several panels of glass that may have been in the Norman church – one is in the second window from the west on the north side of the nave, another at the foot of the Five Sisters window, another is the St Nicholas panel and others are in the nave clerestory windows on the south side. Two treasures still preserved by the Minster which were here in pre-Conquest days are a gospel book and a drinking horn (the latter given as a sign of a gift of property to the cathedral).

FACING PAGE, ABOVE: *The high altar, designed by Sir Walter Tapper in 1938, is a memorial to the second Viscount Halifax. The statues at each end of the screen are (left) King Edwin and (right) King Edward VII. Beyond is the great east window, one of the largest areas of medieval stained glass in a single window in the world. Its panels contain scenes from the Old Testament.*

FACING PAGE, BELOW: *The Zouche Chapel, named after its founder, William de la Zouche, Archbishop of York 1340–52, is reserved for private prayer. The medieval wall cupboards once housed archives and treasures. The two wooden statues of a bishop and the Virgin Mary were placed here in 1944.*

ABOVE: *St Cuthbert's window, in the south choir transept, c. 1440. The donor, Thomas Langley, Bishop of Durham, was formerly Dean of York. The panels below the canopy heads tell the story of St Cuthbert, who was consecrated bishop in the Saxon minster in 685. In the lower part is a large central figure of the saint, holding the head of St Oswald, which was buried with him in Durham Cathedral.*

The Present Minster

The present building was begun in the 1220s and took 250 years to complete. None of the men who began, and very few of those who continued the work could ever have hoped to see their handiwork finished. The initiative came from Walter de Gray, archbishop from 1216 until his death in 1255, and a leading figure in the government of England in the reign of Henry III. His splendid thirteenth-century tomb is on the east side of the south transept. When it was dismantled in 1968 in order to be rebuilt securely, a stone coffin was uncovered at ground level. The lid, painted with the representation of an archbishop in full vestments, and the chalice, paten, ring and crozier contained inside the coffin, are preserved in the Treasury of the Minster. In the ceiling above the tomb may be seen a contemporary boss of St Michael.

The two transepts, north and south, were built in the middle years of the thirteenth century and finished probably about 1260. They are in the Early English style of architecture, with piers of clustered shafts, varied with columns of Purbeck marble, and each has a well-defined triforium. They replaced the narrower Norman transepts and set the scale for the rest of the new building. The spaciousness resulting from its great size is one of the chief beauties of York Minster. The arches of the central tower are 90 feet (27.5m) high, the height to the inside wooden vaulting 184 feet (56m), the length of the whole building from east to west 486 feet (148m) and the breadth across the transepts from north to south 223 feet (68m).

The tower of the thirteenth-century minster had the same ground area as the present one. It lasted until 1407 when, on a stormy night, it collapsed and was rebuilt in the current Perpendicular style. There had been, and there was to continue to be, a history of trouble with the central tower. It seems likely that it was intended to surmount it with a spire, but that the risk was considered to be too great. Visitors often ask about the relative heights of central and western towers: in fact the topmost pinnacle of the western towers are 18 inches (46cm) higher than the parapet of the central tower.

The chief glory of the north transept is the window in the north wall consisting of five huge lancets, each over 50 feet (15m) high and five feet (1.5m) wide, with patterns of interlacing plant stems on a grisaille background. It is known as the Five Sisters. The glass of the five smaller lancets above is modern, and is designed to match the tone of the thirteenth-century glass beneath. The fine twelfth-century panel at the bottom of the middle light dates from the earlier Norman cathedral and was in the nave clerestory until removed for restoration in the early 1970s.

Among the objects and places of interest in the transepts are the regimental chapels, furnished after the First World War, remarkable for their Renaissance-style marble altars which go so well with their Gothic setting, and the superb modern wrought-iron grilles, reminiscent of a characteristic feature of Spanish cathedrals, the exquisite Victorian monument of Dean Duncombe in the south transept and the post-Second World War astronomical clock in the north, near the entrance to the chapter house.

The chapter house, in the purest Decorated style, was the next part of the present building to be begun. The background to the building history of chapter house and nave (begun 1291) was provided by the comings and goings of Edward I and his armies and government departments during the Scottish wars. On occasions the chapter house was used by the royal chancery, and York was a seat of government for the whole country. The baronial shields on the walls of the nave are a reminder of this history. The chapter house was much admired by an unknown visitor whose words are painted on the wall just inside the door, '*ut rosa flos florum sic est domus ista domorum*', as the rose is the best of flowers so this is the best of buildings. It was meant to have a stone roof and a central pillar, but in fact has neither. The roof is of wood, and a scale model (1954) illustrates the structure of the medieval timbers. The carved figures and foliage of the canopied stalls are especially beautiful, and the windows, except for some panels in the window facing the door and the shields of the tracery, are contemporary with the building. The outside of the chapter house was completed during the 1360s. The present vestibule connecting the chapter house to the north transept was added during the building of the nave and chapter house. The carvings of the chapter house were renewed, the building restored and a floor of Minton tiles laid in 1844–5. The monument of the principal benefactor, Dr Stephen Beckwith, is in the north choir aisle.

The west wall of the nave was finished in 1338; and the roof in the 1350s. The central span of the roof is of wood, the aisle vaulting of stone. Some of the chief stylistic differences between nave and transepts are to be seen in the design of the pillars, the arcading round the inside walls and the shape and size of the

FACING PAGE, ABOVE: *The 15th-century font in the eastern crypt is sited at the head of what may have been a well, now filled in, which is by tradition the place where King Edwin was baptized on Easter Eve, 627. The elaborate font cover was designed by Sir Ninian Compter in 1946. The figures are, from left, Queen Ethelburga, King Edwin, Bishop Paulinus, St Hilda and James the Deacon.*

FACING PAGE, BELOW: *The York Virgin. This damaged bas-relief of the Virgin and Child in the eastern crypt was found buried in a cavity in the east wall of the Minster in 1923. It is thought to date from the 12th century, and was possibly originally mounted above the altar of the Lady Chapel. The deliberate mutilation of the heads probably occurred during the period of violent Protestantism during the archi-episcopate of Archbishop Holgate in the mid-1500s.*

ABOVE: *The eastern crypt, the oldest part of the building. The photograph shows the Romanesque carved capitals and modern paintings of SS Paulinus, Hilda and Edwin.*

RIGHT: *The shrine of St William, in the western crypt. The mosaic pavement surrounding the sarcophagus represents the swirling waters of the Ouse. Like the wall-hanging beyond, it was designed and made in 1980 by students at the York College of Art.*

windows. The triforium has been virtually eliminated, for it is little more than an ornamented support for the clerestory windows. The windows of the north and south nave aisles are nearly all from the early fourteenth century. The west window (1338) has remarkable curvilinear tracery in a design which suggests the shape of a heart. Although it is nowadays known popularly as 'the heart of Yorkshire', it is likely that it originally reflected a particular devotion to the humanity of Christ that was beginning to be practised at the time. There are remains of fourteenth-century carvings on the west walls, all save the northernmost from the biblical story of Samson, and modern sculptured figures near the west doors. The doors themselves are early Victorian work, replacing the doors that perished in a fire of 1840. A doorway on the north wall of the nave near the west end once led to an earlier (Norman) chapel which has since disappeared.

The choir was begun after 1360 at the east end and finished in the early 1400s. The style is Perpendicular, apparently adapted to match the nave. The easternmost part, the Lady Chapel, was built by John Thoresby, archbishop 1352-73. To the north of this area is the tomb of Richard Scrope, the archbishop who in 1405 was executed (or, as Yorkshire people thought, murdered) by order of Henry IV after taking part in an unsuccessful rebellion. A cult of St Richard Scrope sprang up in the north, books of hours in the Minster Library are to be found which contain prayers addressed to him, and the westernmost window in the south choir aisle registers the silent protest of the Dean and Chapter against the act. Every scene of martyrdom gives a prominent place to the persecuting secular power. To the north of the Lady Chapel is St Stephen's Chapel, with a fine mid-Victorian reredos behind the altar, and on the south side the chapel (All Saints') of the Duke of Wellington's Regiment with modern wrought-iron screens. Further westwards the two great Perpendicular 'walls of glass' north and south of the choir illuminated the high altar, which, until 1726, stood one bay further west than it does now. Behind it was the shrine of St William, whose life is commemorated in the northern window.

On the south side of the choir, entered from the aisle, is the Zouche Chapel, reserved for private prayer. This was endowed by the archbishop of that name in 1352, and rebuilt in the early sixteenth century. The east window is noticeably off-centre, and the reason for this is plain if the building is

Continued on page 18

FACING PAGE, ABOVE: *The south choir aisle has some fine monuments, especially that of William Gee (1611), a lawyer of the Council of the North, and those of Archbishop Lamplugh (1688–91) and Archbishop Dolben (1683–6) by Grinling Gibbons.*

FACING PAGE, BELOW: *All Saints, chapel of the Duke of Wellington's Regiment, at the east end of the south choir aisle. The mid-14th-century window is made up of brilliant fragments surrounding a figure of St James of Compostella.*

ABOVE: *The Lady Chapel. The coloured stone reredos commemorates the reign of Queen Victoria. On the right is the tomb of Archbishop Bowet (d. 1423). The late 18th-century oak pews, previously in the Acton Almshouses of the Goldsmiths' Company, were restored in 1979.*

RIGHT: *The tomb of Archbishop Richard Scrope. Miracles were believed to have happened here immediately after his execution in 1405, which, combined with regional patriotism, caused him to be acclaimed as a saint.*

The Enthronement of the Archbishop of York

On 18 November 1983 the Right Reverend John Habgood, formerly Bishop of Durham, was enthroned in the Minster as the 95th Lord Archbishop of York, Primate of England. The photograph above, taken just after the enthronement, shows the Archbishop being led to the nave to be presented with the pastoral staff and welcomed by representatives of the Church and community. He is preceded by the Dean of York, the Very Reverend Ronald Jasper; the Head Verger, Mr Richard Bunday, and the Archbishop's Chaplain, the Reverend Simon Wright (with the primatial cross). Behind him is the Archbishop's Lay Chaplain, Mr David Blunt. On the high altar can be seen a magnificent display of some of the Minster's treasures, including alms dishes, chalices, prayer books and bibles.

In the photograph on the left, the Archbishop is holding his own staff, which he leaves at the altar before receiving the silver pastoral staff. This has been in the Minster with little interruption since 1688 and is normally displayed in the Treasury.

★

FACING PAGE: *The nave, looking west. The timber projecting from the triforium on the right may once have supported the chain of a medieval font cover.*

looked at from the outside, where it can be seen how a section of the wall is taken up by one of the buttresses of the choir. The iron fittings of the cupboards in the chapel are fourteenth-century, and the two stalls near the altar are the only ones remaining from the fire of 1829 which destroyed all the other woodwork in the choir. There is a well at the west end, one of many in the area. There are two rooms to the west, the first a sacristy (formerly a treasury) and the next a consistory court, used also as a sacristy. The door into the sacristy from the aisle is a fine example of Victorian carving, designed by Bodley, the architect, and executed by H. R. and W. Franklin (1891).

The rebuilding of the choir was rounded off by the choir screen (1475–1500). It was the work of William Hyndeley, and the statues of kings of England from William the Conqueror are contemporary with the screen, except for the last, of Henry VI, which dates from 1810. The vaulting of the choir entrance contains a delicate boss of the Blessed Virgin, recoloured in 1930. The walls of the choir were cleaned and the ceiling painted and gilded in 1970–1.

Too often visitors are so anxious to enter the building that they do not take sufficient notice of the beauty and interest of the external fabric. The deeply recessed windows of the choir, the parapet round the roof, the east wall leaning out nearly two feet (60cm), the varied styles of the western towers and the carved figures on the exterior all repay attention. The western towers were an afterthought, which probably accounts for the inadequacy of their foundations before the recent repairs. The south-west tower was finished in 1456, the north-west in 1474 and the central tower in 1480. On 3 July 1472 a re-dedication of the practically completed building was carried out, and the date has since been observed as marking the end of the 250 years' task.

The Windows

The Minster and the parish churches of York are famous for their medieval glass. Between them they contain the greatest single concentration of medieval stained and painted glass in the country, and the Minster's windows rank with those of Chartres in quality and quantity. In the later Middle Ages there was a flourishing school of glass painters in York, and many of the windows in the Minster were its products. The elaborate canopies enshrining single figures of saints help to unite the glass with the architecture, and the use

18

of yellow stain gives the windows great brilliance. Some of the borders are full of unexpected details, for example at the bottom of the fifth window from the west on the north side of the nave, where there are portrayed a cock reading a lesson, a monkey's funeral, a fox stealing a hen and a hunt. The east window of the choir is one of the largest expanses of stained glass in the world and a supreme achievement of Gothic art. It was the work of John Thornton of Coventry (who has left his signature towards the top of the window) between 1405 and 1408. God the Father, Alpha and Omega, presides in the top tracery light over the ranks of saints and angels. Then come three rows of Old Testament subjects beginning with the days of creation; below them the main part of the window illustrates the last book of the Bible, the *Revelation of St John*, and the bottom row consists of bishops and kings.

There is glass of every century from the twelfth to the twentieth. The earlier windows give the effect of rich mosaics; sixteenth-century ones, like the easternmost of the choir aisles on each side (which are French), are more concerned to tell a story and look like contemporary oil paintings. Contrasting greatly with the medieval glass, but good of its kind in colour and design, and of great historical interest, is the work of the eighteenth-century York glass painter William Peckitt. Four of his windows are in the south wall of the south transept, two each side of the door, and there are examples of his work in the tracery of some of the nave windows. He was also responsible for

Continued on page 22

★

FACING PAGE, ABOVE: *The altar of St Stephen's Chapel, at the east end of the north choir aisle, was originally the high altar and is remarkable for the 19th-century terracotta panel in the reredos. The sea-green frontal is of 18th-century embroidered Chinese silk.*

FACING PAGE, BELOW: *The tomb of Archbishop Thomas Savage (d. 1507). It was originally surmounted by a wooden chantry chapel, which was restored in 1949 to a design by Sir Albert Richardson.*

ABOVE RIGHT: *The mural monument of Sir Henry Belasyse. Sir Henry, who died in 1630, ordered the monument for himself and his wife from the sculptor Nicholas Stone. The young man at the base became Lord Fauconberg, whose son married Oliver Cromwell's daughter Mary.*

RIGHT: *Effigy of Prince William of Hatfield (Yorks.), who died in childhood. He was the son of Edward III, who was married in the Minster in 1328.*

ABOVE LEFT: *The Five Sisters window, c.1250, is one of the earliest windows in the Minster still in its original place, the north transept. Each of the lights of grisaille glass with coloured accents has a different design. The more brightly coloured panel at the bottom of the central light is from the Norman minster and depicts Daniel in the lion's den.*

ABOVE: *The astronomical clock in the north transept (1955) is a memorial to the airmen of Britain, the Commonwealth and allies, who, operating from bases in the north-east, died during the Second World War.*

LEFT: *The St Nicholas Chapel in the north transept is a children's chapel. The rich altar frontal is embroidered with the legend of St Nicholas and there is a wooden statue of the saint above the altar. The kneelers depict the twelve days of Christmas. On the right is the tomb and brass of Archbishop Greenfield (d. 1315). Behind it is the only remaining piece of medieval carved screenwork in the Minster, the rest having been destroyed in the 1829 fire. The modern painted panel depicts a scene from the life of St Nicholas and is based on an Annunciation by Carlo Crivelli in the National Gallery.*

FACING PAGE: *The 13th-century chapter house is still used for meetings of the Dean and Chapter; also, nowadays, for concerts and exhibitions. The painted ceiling (top) was restored by John Carr in 1798 and repainted in 1976.*

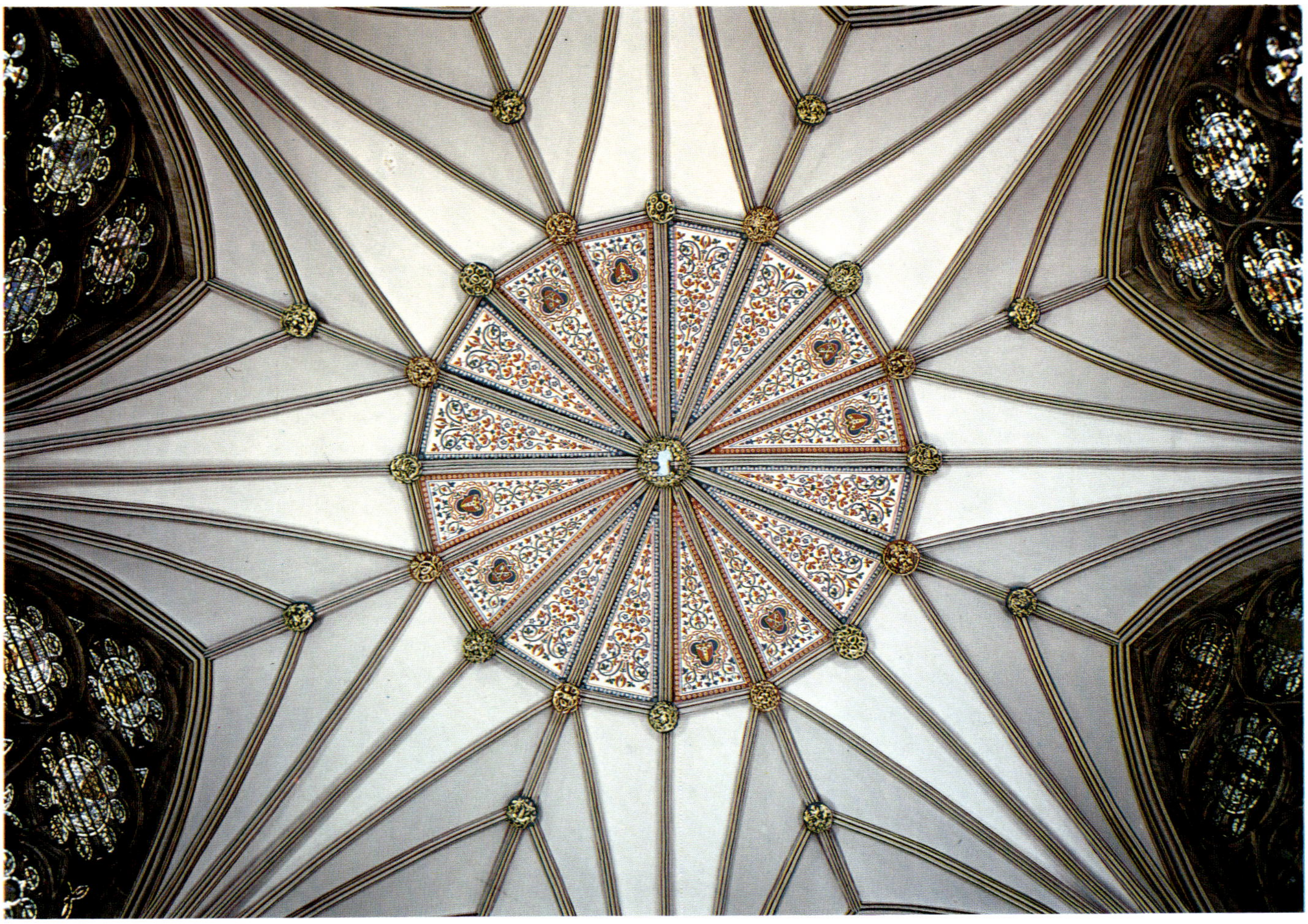

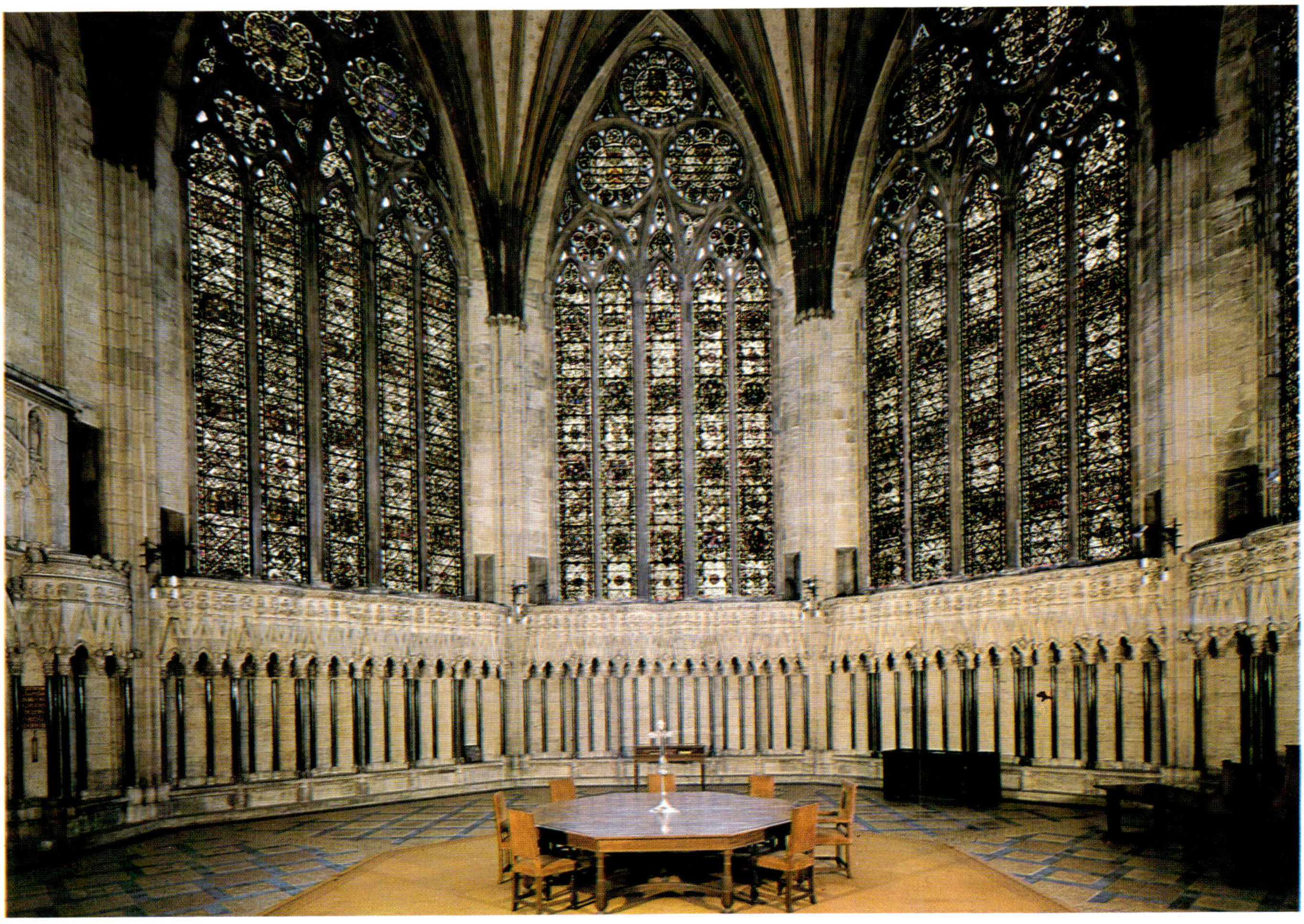

the acquisition of one of the windows from New College, Oxford, now in the south choir aisle.

Many of the windows were taken out for safety during the First World War, and a considerable programme of restoration was undertaken in the 1920s. In 1939 most of the older windows were removed, and this time an extensive reordering of the windows was undertaken under the direction of the dean, Eric Milner-White. Many of the windows had become, through unskilful restoration in previous centuries, badly jumbled and the work of getting them back to their original condition resembled the effort to solve a gigantic jigsaw puzzle. In 1967, with the aid of the Pilgrim Trust, a Glaziers' Trust was set up to undertake the repair of good glass from any source, but with the care of the Minster glass as the first call on its skill. The repair of the glass and, where necessary, its reordering proceeds with the best scholarly advice available and as funds allow. The glass of York Minster is a great artistic treasure which the Dean and Chapter hold in trust for the civilized world.

Later History

The fabric and glass were preserved from damage during the siege of York in 1644 thanks to the Parliamentary general Lord Fairfax. The city undertook the care of the fabric during the Commonwealth and provided (Puritan) preachers. The seventeenth century was a great age of monumental sculpture, and there is a fine array of monuments in the choir aisles and at the east end. Some of the coloured marble and alabaster effigies of the early part of the century and the white marble figures of mitred archbishops from the later part are especially notable. There are two, possibly three, by Grinling Gibbons (Archbishops Sterne, Dolben and Lamplugh). The floor of the nave was re-laid between 1731 and 1734 under the direction of Richard Boyle, third Earl of Burlington. The pattern was reproduced when new stones were laid in 1971–2. The early eighteenth-century wrought-iron gates of the choir and choir aisles are of delicate beauty. There is some interesting carved stonework by the local family of the Fishers during the eighteenth century, for example the monument to Sir George Savile (d. 1784), Member of Parliament for the County of York.

In 1829 and again in 1840 there were destructive fires which entailed much subsequent restoration. The first, which gutted the choir, was caused deliberately by Jonathan Martin, who was later found to be insane. The restoration, including the provision of entirely new choir stalls, copied from the previous ones, took three years. Sir Robert Smirke designed the teak roof and vaulted ceiling, the throne, pulpit and choir stalls, organ case and the stone screen behind the altar. The second fire was caused by the accident of a workman's candle left burning in the south-west tower and badly damaged the nave. The architect of the restoration, 1840–4, was Smirke's brother Sydney, who designed the roof and pine ceiling. The bosses were copied with great exactness from the fourteenth-century ones carved by Philip of Lincoln, thanks to the forethought of the local historian John Browne, who had made careful drawings of them after the earlier fire.

In the later Victorian period much careful restoration was done and many works of great beauty added. G. E. Street not only renewed the buttresses of the triforium and the gables and pinnacles over the entrance of the south transept but also designed the monument of Dean Duncombe inside it. He designed (for the choir sanctuary) the altar now in St Stephen's Chapel and George Tinworth made the terracotta panel, *The first hour of the Crucifixion*, as a reredos. From 1882 to 1907 G. F. Bodley was the consulting architect to the Dean and Chapter. Among his contributions are the stone statues on the piers of the Lady Chapel and the reredos on the east wall (the Minster's commemoration of Queen Victoria) and the flying buttresses of the nave, replacing ones removed in the eighteenth century. He was succeeded by Walter Tapper, to whom many of the chapels as well as the choir sanctuary owe their present appearance. In conjunction with an inspired craftsman in metal, Bainbridge Reynolds, he designed the impressive wrought-iron screens and the altars in the three regimental chapels. He began the re-ordering of the choir sanctuary and the design of a completely new high altar, a memorial to Charles Lindley Wood, second Viscount Halifax.

The work was completed after his death by his successor, Charles Peers, who was responsible for the excavations in the crypt in 1931 and the preparation of the eastern crypt for use. Little ancient woodwork survived the fires of the nineteenth century, but the loss has been supplied by an abundance of modern work. Ninian Comper is represented by a font cover in the crypt and a pulpit in the nave; Albert Richardson, Peers' successor, by a nave throne, a gospel ambo in the choir sanctuary and a reconstructed chantry over the Savage monument in the north choir aisle. The ceiling of the north transept was renewed between 1934 and 1951. An astronomical clock, the united work of architect, artist and engineer (Richardson, H. J. Stammers, R. d'E. Atkinson) was placed in the north transept in 1955. In 1963 work was completed on the little Our Father Chapel (in the nave) named after the oldest of the city guilds. The designer was Francis Johnson, and the wrought iron, containing the *chi rho*, Constantine's symbol of Christ, was made by W. Dowson. Extensive repairs to the external stone-work were carried out after the Second World War.

In 1967 an appeal for two million pounds was launched to save the building from collapse, and in the course of a five-year restoration programme massive new foundations were supplied to the central tower, and to the east and west ends of the building. The opportunity was taken to clean the interior thoroughly and to begin the cleaning of the outside. With special grants from the city and from the Friends of the Minster the ceilings were cleaned and the bosses painted and gilded. The architect for the work was Bernard Feilden. The eleventh Earl of Scarborough, who led the appeal and who died in 1969, is commemorated by a stone immediately under the central tower.

★

FACING PAGE, LEFT: *The Bellfounders' window, in the north aisle, dates from the early 1300s and was given by Richard Tunnoc, a goldsmith and bellfounder who was buried in the Minster in 1330. The lower panels show the craft of bell-making, tuning and casting, and the central panel, illustrated here, depicts the donor presenting a model of the window to St William of York.*

FACING PAGE, RIGHT: *The King's Own Yorkshire Light Infantry Chapel of St John in the north transept. The Italianate marble altar and the wrought-iron grille, designed by Sir Walter Tapper, were added in 1925.*

RIGHT: *The south transept, built about 1240 in Early English style, and the central tower, built in the 15th century in Perpendicular style after the collapse of the earlier bell-tower.*

The Undercroft

The Undercroft came into being as a consequence of the near disaster of the winter of 1966-7 when grave weakness was discovered in the foundations of the central tower, affecting its stability and therefore the safety of the whole building. In order that the engineers might explore the foundations of the four great piers which were yielding under their load, and design a modern reinforcement for them, thousands of tons of soil and rubble were removed from beneath the tower and the adjacent areas (the two transepts, the two easternmost bays of the nave and the western ends of the choir aisles: the Norman crypt under the present choir had been cleared after the fire of 1829 and was now linked with this newly created space). For five years there went on, in the full gaze of the visiting public (which had to traverse this part of the Minster on specially constructed wooden bridges) the work of excavation, shoring and ballasting, transporting and pouring concrete, drilling, grouting and reinstating. The strength of the foundations was doubled, and the awe-inspiring cliffs of concrete, bound to the old masonry by stainless steel rods, and surrounding the old foundations of the four piers like gigantic collars, form the principal exhibit of the new Undercroft and its *raison d'être*.

Engineering and Archaeology

Long before the work began it had been known that this was a site of great historical importance and likely to be rich in archaeological material. As mentioned above in the section on the Minster's early history, the Minster stands on the central part of a Roman legionary fortress which had been the most important military centre in the north of Roman Britain. How much of its administrative headquarters remained, and what happened to the buildings after the Romans left? Later, we know from unforgettable pages in the Venerable Bede, there was a stone Saxon church: perhaps exploration would yield evidence of it. Later still came the Vikings, and with them the increasing commercial importance of York: would any trace have been left of their use of the Roman building? It was known that remains of the Norman church underlay (and some, perhaps, were encased in) the present building, but its dimensions were unknown. Much was obscure in the architectural history of the minster of the 1070s onwards, of its extension and rebuilding in the twelfth and thirteenth centuries and the relation it bore to the present building. It was un-

TOP: *A model of the headquarters building* (principia) *of the Roman fortress which once stood on this site. It was built for the Ninth Legion late in the 1st or early 2nd century* AD, *but was mostly occupied by the Sixth. In all it covered about 50 acres and housed 5,600 heavy infantry. The* principia *was the centre of the whole area, and from its cross-hall* (basilica), *seen on the far side, the province of northern Britain* (Britannia Inferior) *was governed. The walls were still standing in Saxon times.*

CENTRE: *Part of a wall-painting from the Roman* principia *reassembled from plaster fragments found lying inside the building.*

BOTTOM: *A Roman stone commemorating a soldier. It was incorporated into the foundation raft of the Norman church.* Collegium *probably refers to a burial club. The lower line mentions the various posts he held, ending with* corricularius *(trumpeter).*

FACING PAGE: *Roman pottery objects, including flagons, bowls and platters, found during the 1967-72 restoration work.*

thinkable that the opportunity afforded by the need for extensive excavations should be not taken. Further, the engineers were aware that they were working in four dimensions. In addition to designing new foundations, they needed to know how their predecessors had built below ground, and there was need therefore for the most careful measurement, photography and sifting of the evidence afforded by stone and soil. In short, they needed archaeologists to help them do their own job, and there followed the most exciting collaboration of the two professions in modern times.

Thanks to their combined efforts the visitor takes a journey through time from the first to the twentieth century. Basically, the area he is visiting is Roman. Before the first Roman troops arrived in A.D. 72 there is no evidence below York Minster of any permanent settlement. From the second century large and splendid buildings stood on a north-east/south-west axis on the area covered now by the Minster and its environs. In the Undercroft the visitor walks in and out of the cross-hall of the *principia*. The hall in itself has a 230 feet (70m) frontage, and was as big as the present transepts and central crossing together. To the north-west, under the nave, lay buildings which may have been barrack blocks; north-east, under the choir and beyond, possibly the commandant's house. One of the results yielded by investigation is that these buildings did not cease to be used after the withdrawal of the legion; another is that the area itself has been continuously occupied, for one purpose or another, from that day to this. No evidence has been forthcoming concerning a Saxon church, but Saxon carved stones have been found *in situ*, and, in a Saxon graveyard discovered under the

★

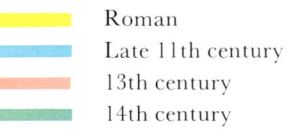
Roman
Late 11th century
13th century
14th century

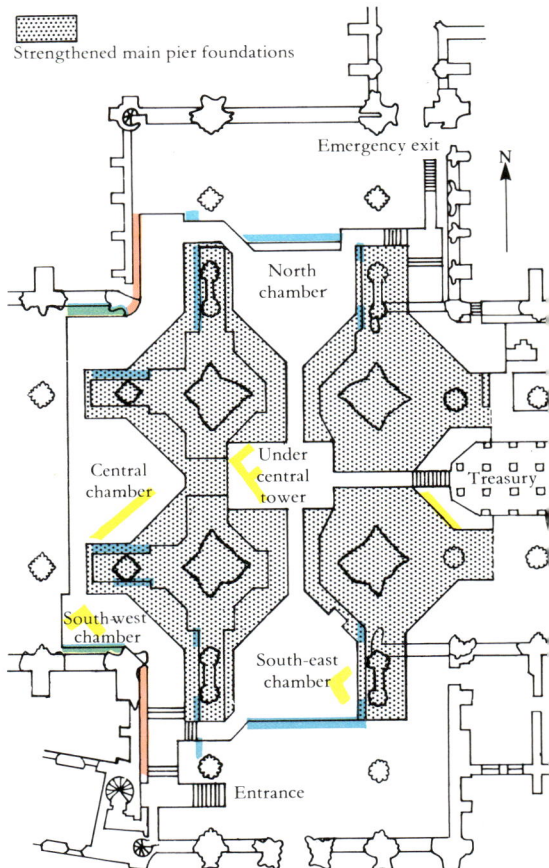

south choir aisle and part of the south transept, gravestones parallel to the Roman axis. The Normans, in the 1070s, began to build a completely new church, deliberately forsaking the existing alignment and building east-west. Their great boldness is made abundantly clear by this disregard of the orientation of the massive buildings that were there before them. The present Minster naturally followed this pattern, and where feasible it was built on Norman foundations but on a greatly enlarged scale. Part of the weakness in the foundations discovered in recent years was due to the fact that the older foundations were not strong enough to bear the weight of the larger building.

A Walk round the Undercroft

As you walk round the area you will be looking at the remains from many different architectural periods: Roman, Norman, Gothic and modern. At some points it is possible to see remains of all four periods at once, and this can be bewildering. Movable exhibits, however, are carefully arranged so far as possible in a chronological order, beginning with the Roman period and progressing through Saxon, Danish, Norman and later medieval to the present. You are with the whole past the whole time, and this can be an exhilarating experience. To make the most of it you need to orient yourself with regard to space and time. As you take the route outlined in this guide check your bearings every now and then with reference to the building above you. Notices and plans at certain points of your tour will help, and this guide book will tell you where you are. You make a circular tour, entering from the south transept, going to the areas under the eastern part of the nave, the north transept, the central tower, the western part of the choir and back to the south transept. As you go, look first at the script on the hanging boards, the first of which faces you as you enter the armoured glass gates at the foot of the steps in the south transept: it gives simple background information, illustrated from time to time by maps and plans, of York's history over nineteen centuries. It is York's history as well as the Minster's for this is the area that gave York its initial importance and which provided the occasion for the city's later growth. The continuous script on the boards links what you are looking at with the development of the city, and suggests its place in the great western civilization, first Roman and classical, then medieval and Christian, to which it belonged. The smaller, standing notices describe the actual objects you are seeing, and relate them to the history of the buildings of the site, around and above you. The aims of both sets of notices, and of the selection of objects for display, are to give an experience of the past and to help towards a better understanding of the great building which towers above you.

You enter by a flight of steps in the south transept. In the reception there faces you the foundation of the west wall of this transept (*c*.1220). As you pass through the armoured glass doors notice on your right part of the west wall of the Norman transept (*c*.1070) the external surface of which, of re-used Roman stone, was covered with plaster, and the masonry joints indicated in red. Already, on the threshold of the Undercroft, you have a glimpse further beneath you of the new concrete collar round the south-west pier. This is approached by another stairway, and from a wooden bridge beyond this you get your first sight of substantial remains of the Roman fortress. At this point the floor level is that of Roman times, and is 12 feet 6 inches (3.8m) below the present floor level of the south aisle of the nave above. In this small, irregularly shaped south-western chamber of the Undercroft, bounded by the concrete collar, the dark red painted concrete containing wall built under the nave, and the lower part of the Norman foundations of the nave, is a piece of the north-east wall of the cross-hall or basilica of the *principia* (second century). At this point you are actually within the hall.

Another wooden bridge leads to a much larger central chamber which contains a wall which is part of an extension to the headquarters building made in the fourth century. On the inside of this particular office room was

★

ABOVE LEFT: *Part of a cross carved in late Saxon times, showing the interlacing typical of that period.*

LEFT: *A painted reconstruction of the De Gray coffin lid, c.1255. The original is on display in the Treasury.*

FACING PAGE, ABOVE: *The north chamber of the Undercroft, showing the modern coffered ceiling, the inside face of the Norman transept wall on the left, medieval bosses, a sarcophagus, and statues from the west front of the Minster.*

FACING PAGE, BELOW: *A 13th-century well, formerly outside the north wall of the Norman nave, and a 13th-century buttress, originally external, now encased by the 14th-century foundations of the present nave.*

the plaster now displayed separately on a board on the west side of the chamber. The plaster (early fourth century) was discovered in fragments at the foot of the wall. These, and the many other Roman remains discovered under the Minster and in areas adjacent to it, notably the reconstructed column found toppled under the south transept, and now standing outside the south door, give a vivid impression of the scale of the building.

The route from the central chamber leads northwards towards the area under the north transept. Here is a complicated set of archaeological remains *in situ* which the notices explain. On one side is a thirteenth-century well which was outside, in the angle of the north wall of the Norman nave and the west wall of the contemporary transept, and was engulfed in subsequent enlargement of the building; and on the other, evidence of the building and rebuilding of the present transept, including above eye level a remarkably unweathered external buttress now encased in later masonry. Saxon carved stones of the eleventh century are collected together, for convenience, in the next area of the Undercroft.

There is some evidence from Minster archaeology that already in early Saxon times industry was carried on amid the buildings of the Roman fortress. The Vikings made York a great commercial centre. Already it was an ecclesiastical centre, thanks partly to the fact that Pope Gregory the Great, probably recalling what he had read of Roman Britain, decided to make York the northern capital of Christianity, matching London in the south; and partly to the place York and its school came to occupy in the Northumbrian culture. The Normans reasserted York's importance in both respects, and with magisterial confidence built the largest stone church north of the Alps in its time on an alignment which ignored not only that of the Roman fortress but also the entire surviving Roman street plan. In the next large area of the Undercroft, the north chamber, amid the concrete foundations, is assembled a number of exhibits to illustrate the history of the Minster in Norman and later times. They will vary from time to time, but the visitor will see a selection of such objects as carved wooden bosses from the Minster's medieval roofs, medieval statuary from the exterior of the present building, and panels of stained and painted glass either from the Minster's own windows (in transit from repair at the workshop of the Glaziers' Trust back to their place) or on loan from other sources. The direct way out is by the corridor between the new foundations, southwards across the area immediately under the central tower into the final south-east chamber, which contains more Roman remains, a temporary exhibition varied from time to time, and a plaque commemorating the principal donors who have helped to set up and furnish this display area in the Undercroft.

The Treasury

No visitor, however, is likely to want to take the shortest way out. From the area under the central tower a flight of steps ascends to the crypt of the old Norman minster, immediately under the westernmost part of the present choir. If the time is between four and five in the afternoon the distant sounds of Evensong are likely to be heard from above, and they complete the magical effect which this mysterious, shadowy space among the reconstructed nineteenth-century arches creates. In this area, bounded at the far end by beautiful modern screens of stainless steel, and at the nearer, west end by the massive steel balcony overlooking a dramatic view seven feet (2m) below of yet another section of the Roman headquarters' walls, treasure of great value and age is displayed. In the first case on your left is a collection of church pewter. The next two contain a unique private collection of York domestic silver from 1485 till 1858. From then onwards the perimeter cases display church plate, either from the Minster's own collection or on loan from the owners, arranged in chronological order. The great central case

★

FACING PAGE, ABOVE: *Commemorative pieces presented to the Minster on the occasion of the restoration celebrations. A thanksgiving service was held on 3 July 1972, 500 years from the day of its consecration.*

FACING PAGE, BELOW: *The interior of the Treasury, looking west, showing the Roman wall, arches reconstructed in the early 19th century after the 1829 fire, and the modern concrete and steel foundations.*

ABOVE RIGHT: *The Treasury, showing part of the central case presented by the Goldsmiths' Company of London, which contains a fine collection of Minster plate and other plate belonging to local churches, on loan to the Dean and Chapter.*

RIGHT: *The Horn of Ulph is a type of drinking vessel made from an elephant tusk and known as an 'oliphant'. It is about a thousand years old, but the silver mountings are 17th-century. The horn was presented to the Minster as a token of a gift of land before the Norman Conquest.*

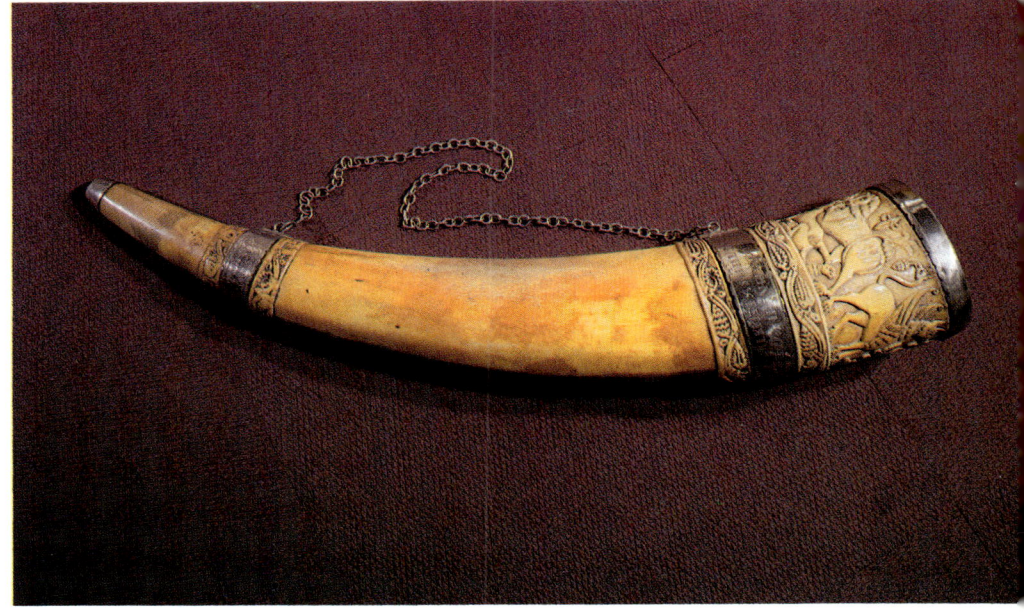

29

consists almost entirely of items of silver and silver-gilt on loan from other sources, mostly from parish churches of the north of England, with rare and interesting pieces from the Roman Catholic Church, the Free Churches and the Scottish Episcopal Church. The oldest item of all is the horn of Ulph, of elephant's tusk, presented nearly a thousand years ago to the Saxon minster. Beyond the steel screens at the back of the Treasury lies the western crypt, which may be entered, with a guide, from the south choir aisle above. In the southwest corner of the Treasury, on your left as you leave, notice the coffin lid with the painted effigy of Archbishop Walter de Gray, who died in 1255, and items from his tomb.

The Message of the Undercroft

Few cathedrals possess an area such as this, and it would not have been brought into being but for the vision and skill of those concerned with the restoration of the fabric, 1967–72, and the generosity of subsequent donors. The names of a few are recorded here, eleven thousand other names of contributors to the fund for saving the building for posterity are inscribed in a volume on display in the north transept. Another volume lies beside it, for the names of those who will give in the future, in order to preserve and continue their achievement. The task of maintaining this great building, like the spiritual task for which it exists, goes on ceaselessly. This display area gives the visitor a glimpse of the heritage that we have received. The Dean and Chapter, who are its guardians, appeal to visitors for financial help in their task of maintaining and enriching it.

★

ABOVE: *The York Gospel Book was made by monks at Canterbury about AD 1000 and brought to York by Wulfstan, Archbishop 1003–23. It contains three full-page illuminations, at the beginning of each of the first three gospels, and is shown open at St Matthew. Deans and other dignitaries have taken their oaths on the book since at least the 13th century, and archbishops probably since 1547. It is kept in the Minster Library.*

FACING PAGE, ABOVE: *The Minster from the east. On the right, with the pointed roof, is the chapter house.*

FACING PAGE, BELOW: *This Roman pillar dating from the 4th century was discovered, toppled, under the south transept and has been re-erected outside the Minster.*

ACKNOWLEDGEMENTS

All the photographs in this book are by Sydney W. Newbery, except the following: Woodmansterne Ltd., front cover (Clive Friend), p. 3 (Nicholas Servian); Aerofilms Ltd., back cover; Sonia Halliday and Laura Lushington, pp. 4, 6 left and top right, 20 top left, 22 right; Fred Spencer, p. 17 top; Press Association, p. 17 bottom; Pickard of Leeds, pp. 21 top, 24 top; B. K. Grayson, p. 32 top. The publishers would also like to thank Derek Phillips, Director of Excavations, York Minster; J. E. Williams and the RHCM (England) for permission to reproduce the replica of the De Gray coffin lid, Messrs. D. J. Dowrick and P. Beckmann of Ove Arup & Partners for permission to use the Undercroft plan, and members of the Minster staff for their help in the preparation of the book.

Designed and produced by Pitkin Pictorials Ltd, 11 Wyfold Road, London SW6 6SG, and printed in Great Britain by Garrod and Lofthouse Ltd, Crawley, Sussex.
© Pitkin Pictorials 1984

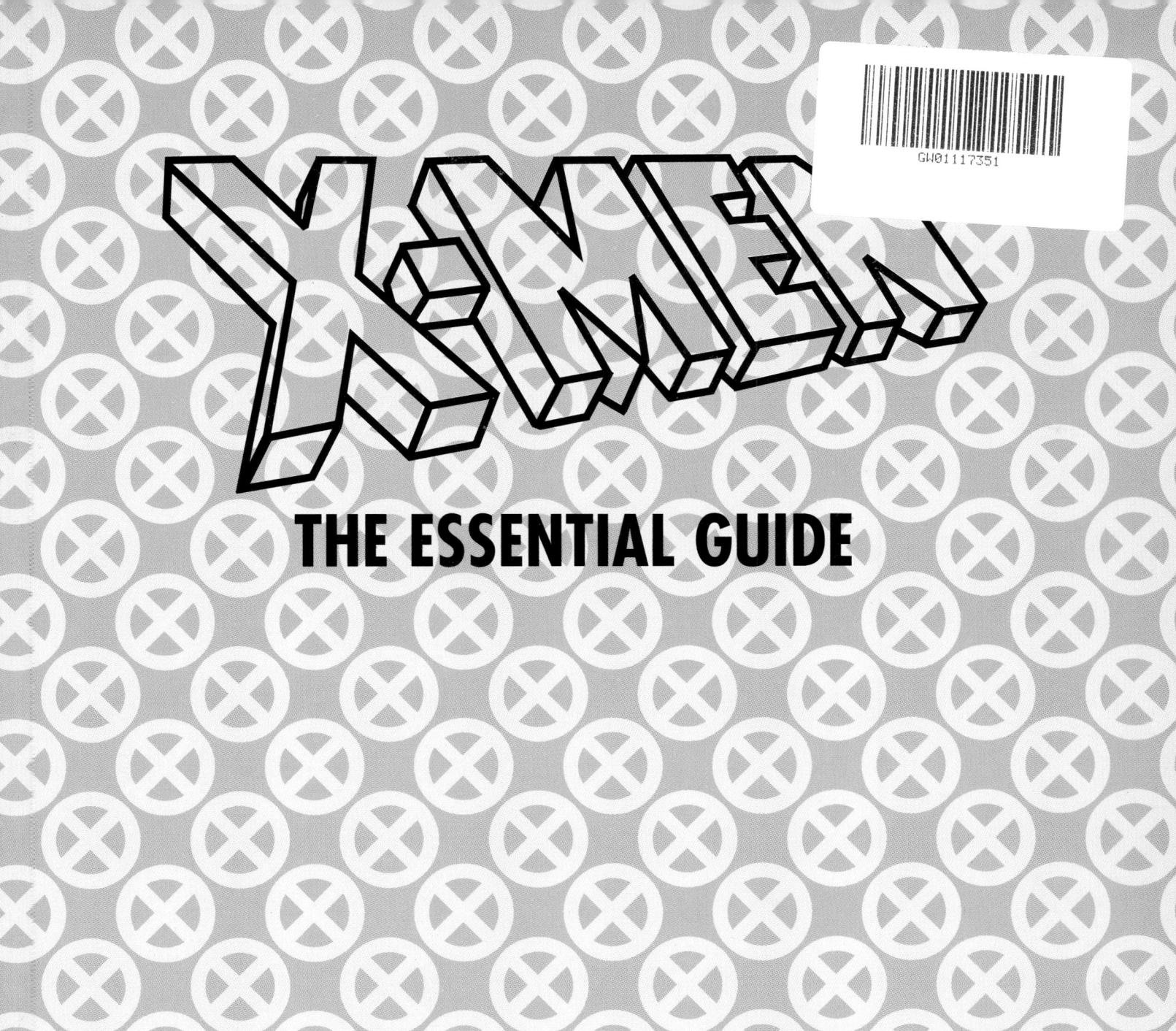

X-MEN

THE ESSENTIAL GUIDE

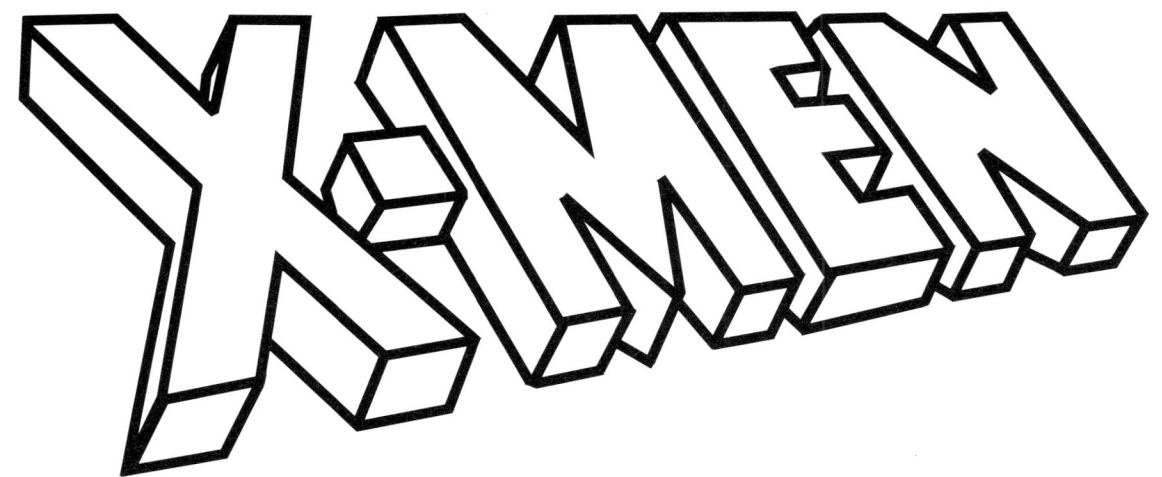

THE ESSENTIAL GUIDE

John Mosby

BOXTREE

First published in Great Britain in 1994 by
Boxtree Limited, Broadwall House, 21 Broadwall, London SE1 9PL

Text copyright © 1994 Boxtree Limited

Illustration copyright © 1994 Marvel Entertainment Group Inc.

All rights reserved.

10 9 8 7 6 5 4 3 2 1

ISBN: 1 85283 394 7   Printed by Rotolito Lombarda Milan

All characters appearing herein and the distinctive names and likenesses thereof are trademarks of Marvel Entertainment Group Inc. No part of this book may be printed or reproduced in any manner without the written permission of the publisher.

Except in the United States of America this book is sold subject to the condition that it shall not, by way of trade or otherwise, be lent, resold, hired out or otherwise circulated without the publisher's prior consent in any form of binding or cover than that in which it is published and without a similar condition including this condition being imposed upon a subsequent purchaser.

Designed and typeset by Blackjacks, London
Identification typeface design by Rian Hughes
Printed and bound in Great Britain by

A CIP catalogue entry for this book is available from the British Library.

BIOS

Archangel	7
Banshee	58
Beast	12
Bishop	13
Cable	16
Changeling	58
Colossus	17
Cyclops	20
Dazzler	58
Excalibur	21
Forge	58
Gambit	25
Havok	58
Iceman	36
Jean Grey	41
Jubilee	49
Longshot	58
Magneto	60
Marvel Girl	41
Mimic	58
Mr Sinister	61
Nightcrawler	58
New Mutants	63
Phoenix II	58
Polaris	58
Professor X	73
Psylocke	76
Rogue	79
Sabretooth	80
Shadowcat	58
Storm	81
Sunfire	58
Thunderbird	58
Wolverine	88

CHAPTERS

Introduction	**6**
History	**8**
the 1960s	8
the 1970s	18
the 1980s	28
the 1990s	50
Inkers and Artists	59
Technicals	**64**
The Mansion:	64
Upper Levels	64
Lower Levels	66
The Danger Room	66
Blackbirds	72
The War Room	74
Cerebro	75
Ready Room	77
Medi-Lab	78
Morlock Tunnels	78
Security	82
Beyond The Mansion	83
Animated Series	**84**
Season 1	86
Season 2	90
And Finally	**92**

INTRODUCTION

Welcome to *The Official X-MEN Handbook*. Some of you will have known the characters in the following pages for many happy years, some will have just jumped on board... no matter — all are welcome.

Marvel has chronicled the adventures of Earth's most uncanny heroes for over thirty years and in that time, millions of people have thrilled to their exploits. Theirs is a story full of tragedy and triumph, failure and success, hate and love... in short, it's about life itself.

Over those thirty years, the faces of the X-MEN have changed, but their outlook and role remain the same. They are any minority you choose to make them, any group of people who are feared and distrusted because they are different, any scapegoat or object of fear. They are ever the underdogs... and we always seem to cheer for the underdogs.

Despite everything man has thrown at them, the various members of the X-MEN have chosen to defend humanity against those who would see them crushed. The X-MEN seek only to live with 'normal' humans in a world that judges by deeds, not appearances. They are heroes for any age.

In the following pages we'll look at their success story and give you some insight into their past and possible future, and talk to some of the people behind their success.

So turn the page... and join the adventure!

BIOGRAPHY

1st Appearance: X-MEN #1

ANGEL
ARCHANGEL

Evidence of Warren Worthington III's mutation first appeared while he was attending an exclusive private school. Small wings began to form on his back and within a few months they had achieved full adult size. Warren managed to keep his new appendages a secret by strapping the wings down against his back. At first he considered himself a 'freak' but began to appreciate the mutation when he realised he could actually use them to fly.

When a fire broke out in the dormitory, he used his wings to rescue some of his classmates. To disguise himself he grabbed a long blonde wig and a nightshirt, which gave him the appearance of an actual angel. His secret was safe and when Warren left the school he adopted the identity of the Avenging Angel and became a crimefighter on the streets of New York City. There he was contacted by Professor Xavier, who recruited him as a founding member of the original X-MEN. For several years Warren remained a member of the team, but left when Xavier recruited new members, including Wolverine who Warren considered a wild liability.

Upon his parents' death, he inherited a vast fortune and created the now-defunct CHAMPIONS. He also revealed his identity to the world, though not his connections to the X-MEN. When the CHAMPIONS failed as an organization, he joined the Beast and Iceman to reorganize the DEFENDERS. When the latter team disbanded, all three members left to join the other original X-MEN team-mates in the first incarnation of X-FACTOR.

During his time with X-FACTOR, the team defended the sewer-dwelling Morlocks, mutant outcasts living under New York City. During an encounter with the Marauders (who were slaughtering the Morlocks), Warren was critically injured and his wings had to be amputated. In the days after the fateful operation, Warren was taken in by the villainous Apocalypse who made him a member of his group The Four Horsemen and gave him the name 'Death'. Apocalypse regrew and augmented Warren's wings, giving them razor-sharp 'feathers' that he could project at will at an adversary. These wings reacted to Warren's emotions, particularly anger. The process also turned his skin blue.

Warren finally managed to turn against Apocalypse and began to try to control his new wings more carefully. He rejoined his original team-mates and returned with them to the X-MEN's mansion to become a member of the Gold Team under the codename Archangel.

HISTORY

THE 1960s

The X-MEN made their debut in September 1963, released as a 12-cent comic book simultaneously with that of the other super-group the AVENGERS. At first a title was published once every two months, though within two years it had reached the monthly schedule it has stayed with since.

The original title for the series, as envisioned by co-creator Stan Lee, was THE MUTANTS but that name was deemed unsuitable and confusing for young readers and so the name X-MEN was chosen. The 'X' does not, as one might think, refer to Charles Xavier's initial, but represents the 'X-Tra' powers that its members were born with.

ORY 4 6 17

Occassionally a cover is passed over for certain design considerations, as was with this Werner Roth cover for X-Men #33. The final version featured a much more dominant image of the unstoppable Juggernaut.

Sometimes an artist creates a look for a character or cover that just doesn't click with what the rest of the creative crew had in mind. Here an unused Werner Roth cover for X-Men #25 was replaced with a piece by original X-co-creator — Jack Kirby.

9

HISTORY

Xavier reads the first outlash against mutants.

In X-MEN #20, Xavier explains how he lost the use of his legs.

The whole idea of 'mutants' was new to Marvel. Most of the characters featuring in other comics were either aliens (à la Superman) or humans endowed with super abilities by some freak quirk of fate (à la Spiderman or the Fantastic Four). The X-MEN's powers were in their genes, present (even if lying dormant) from the moment they were born. Here was the chance for a twist on the conventional super-human stories. Marvel, which had seen the success of highlighting everyday problems for Peter Parker while thrilling to the exploits of alter-ego Spiderman, realised that they could show the problems teenagers faced as well as the *zap, bang, wallop* that readers demanded.

In the first issues, that characterisation — a quality that would eventually make the X-MEN the success they are today — was perhaps a little less evident, but action clashes with other characters (including the AVENGERS) kept readers' interest.

Jack Kirby, one of Marvel's most respected founding fathers, was brought on board the project to work with Stan Lee.

'Jack was the best guy to work with you can imagine,' said Lee. 'Any idea I would give him, he could make it better. When Jack brought in the first story, it opened with all the X-MEN fighting in the place they called the Danger Room, where they were trained. That was Jack's idea... and it was the most brilliant opening because it started with action and showed all their abilities immediately.'

But Jack, whose talents were always in demand, didn't stay with the title for very long and Werner Roth began pencilling the X-MEN over Kirby's layouts.

In the very first issue of the X-MEN, Magneto and his powers are very much in evdence.

THAT "LIVING FENCE" AS YOU CALL IT, IS THE SYMBOL OF MY GREAT POWER! IT IS A MIGHTY SHIELD OF MAGNETIC ENERGY!

AND SO I HAVE NOW ACCOMPLISHED MY FIRST OBJECTIVE! GENTLEMEN, CAPE CITADEL IS MINE!

Biography: BEAST

1st Appearance: X-MEN #1

Henry McCoy's mutant abilities were virtually evident at birth. He possessed larger than normal hands and feet, yet soon proved he could use them with great dexterity.

From his early years, his incredible agility and athletic abilities earned him recognition. These feats attracted the attention of Professor Xavier, who invited 'Hank' to join Xavier's School for Gifted Youngsters where he became one of the founding members of the original X-MEN and was given the codename 'Beast'.

On graduating from the School, Hank joined the private sector as a genetic researcher for the Brand Corporation. After intensive research, McCoy believed he had isolated the chemicals that triggered some mutations. He performed a 'field test' with the serum on himself, hoping it might enable him to track down enemy agents at the research facility. However, the potion made him more animal-like and caused him to sprout blue hair all over his body, grow larger canine teeth and see an increase in his already considerable athletic ability. When Hank remained too long in this form, he realised that he had become trapped and could not return to his more human shape.

Leaving Brand, the Beast joined the AVENGERS and became a full-time adventurer. He later joined the now-defunct DEFENDERS. Later still he joined the original X-MEN to form the first incarnation of X-FACTOR. During this time he was kidnapped by a scientist, Dr Carl Maddicks, and as a side-effect of Maddicks' experiment he reverted to human form. However, an encounter with a mutant, Infectia, a few months later, made the mutation repeat itself and now Hank McCoy is reasonably content in his current animal-like form. When the original X-FACTOR disbanded, he returned with the original X-MEN to Xavier's mansion and became a member of the Blue Team.

McCoy retains his brilliant scientific mind and is a respected expert on genetics. Recently he has begun to question whether he should cultivate his medical talents rather than fighting menaces of a more physical nature alongside his team-mates. He is at the forefront of medical research and is devoting more and more time to a search for cures for diseases, most prominently the Legacy Virus that kills mutants.

BIOGRAPHY
BISHOP

1st Appearance: UNCANNY X-MEN #282

Bishop hails from a possible future timeline where he was a member of the XSE (Xavier Security). Pursuing the mutant Fitzroy, who had released an army of criminals back into the past, Bishop and his fellow soldiers realised too late that the journey 'down-time' was a one-way trip. During the ensuing battle, the X-MEN became involved, unsure of who the real threats were. During the battle Bishop's partners were killed and a handful of criminals (including Fitzroy) escaped. The X-MEN held Bishop for questioning. He revealed to Professor Xavier that he was a soldier from the future, a future inspired by the legend of the X-MEN. He also carried with him a terrible secret. According to a secret recording he had seen in the future, one of the current X-MEN betrays and slays the team at a future date. Professor Xavier decided to keep that information secret from the team. Bishop, who encountered a mystical 'Le Beau' who had once betrayed the X-MEN in his own time, still suspects that the traitor in question could be the Cajun thief Gambit.

The future was a dangerous place to live and a soldier's life was difficult. Bishop learned to fight hard, fast and strong in the defence of the XSE ideals. He has had something of a hard time in learning to hold back his aggressive feelings in a world very different from his own.

Fitzroy remains free and Bishop has sworn to catch up with his nemesis. For the moment, though, he remains with the X-MEN, operating as part of their Gold Team. The irony of living a legend is not lost on this soldier of the future and he lives his life on a day-to-day basis.

With Roth's background in romance comics it could be fair to say that the personal sub-plots (including the Cyclops/Marvel Girl/Angel love triangle) began to sneak in around this time.

Stan also decided, soon after, to move on to other projects.

'I think maybe Jack and I should have stayed with it a little longer, to give it more push,' admits Lee.

Towards the end of Lee and Kirby's run, the adventures of the X-MEN began to overspill the page count and stories were continued in the next issue, or in some cases, several issues later. The style kept readers hooked and racing to get the next issues, wondering how their heroes could survive the latest attack or face more personal challenges. This 'soap-opera syndrome', as Lee jokingly referred to it, seemed like a marketing device to some, but it quickly set precedents that shaped modern comic-publishing strategies.

Even superheroes aren't always prepared for everything.

Old webhead should really have considered the marketing benefits...!

Roy Thomas took on the writing chores in 1966 and stayed with the title until the beginning of the '70s. Thomas had joined Marvel to take on some of the workload. He started out on Millie the Model but soon found himself handling both the X-MEN and the AVENGERS.

'At twenty-five I wasn't that far away from the typical Marvel reader and I sort of knew what they wanted,' admits Thomas.

During the 1960s, the X-MEN had their first encounters with Magneto (#1), the Sentinels (#14) and Polaris (#49), to name but a few, and in the course of those seven years much of the groundwork for the characters and some of their inter-relationships was established.

BIOGRAPHY
CABLE

1st Appearance: (AS ADULT) NEW MUTANTS #87

Cable, on first appearance, seemed to be a mercenary with an extensive arsenal of high-tech weaponry. He took on the might of the Mutant Liberation Front and led the New Mutants for a short time until the creation of X-FORCE. His underlying agenda involved tracking a man named Stryfe (who was his exact duplicate, though this was unknown to Cable at the time) and locating a young man who would in fact become an External. This turned out to be Sam Guthrie (Cannonball — see NEW MUTANTS entry).

Cable's past, or future, depending on which way you choose to look at it, is much more dramatic...

Cable has been revealed to be Nathan Dayspring Askanison, a.k.a. Nathan Christopher Summers, the son of Scott Summers and his first wife Madelyne Pryor. When Apocalypse infected the infant with a deadly techno-virus, Askani (a time traveller sent to that exact time and moment) told Scott that Nathan could be saved in her own time, but would never be able to return. Scott had no choice but to send his son to the future.

There an attempt was made to clone the child in the hope that he would become the predicted leader of their society. It first appeared that Cable was the 'imperfect' clone of Nathan Summers and that his nemesis Stryfe was the 'original' child. Recent revelations seem to suggest that this was in fact a lie (believed by both Cable and Stryfe) and that Cable is the original. Stryfe's mistaken belief led to his wreaking revenge upon his 'parents' Jean and Scott — first through the Mutant Liberation Front and then on a much more personal level.

Finally the X-Teams and Cable fought Stryfe on the Moon and it seemed that both Cable and Stryfe were destroyed. Both, in fact, survived, though their minds now shared one body. When the truth of their origins was revealed Stryfe allowed Cable to resume control of his body... at least for the moment.

Cable continues to fight alongside X-FORCE and on an individual basis. His relationship with Scott, Jean and 'sister' Rachel continues to develop.

1st Appearance: GIANT SIZE X-MEN #1

BIOGRAPHY

COLOSSUS

Piotr (Peter) Rasputin was born on the Ust-Ordynski Soviet Collective Farm in Siberia. As a young teenager he was content to use his awakening mutant ability (to change his skin to an organic metal) to help the farmers and the State.

When Professor Xavier told him of his desire to create a second generation of X-MEN, Peter agreed to help, believing the Professor's argument that mutant abilities should be used for a greater good. After saving the lives of the original X-MEN, Peter found that he could not be content with farm life and remained with the team. He became a mainstay of this second generation, his strength and invulnerability in battle tempered by his artistic soul. Peter, perhaps more than anybody, believed in the X-MEN's values. He refused to take a life, even if his own was at stake.

But times change and life for the X-MEN rarely got any easier. Time and time again, they were forced to choose between two evils. When the Morlocks were slaughtered in the sewers below New York City, the X-MEN were also attacked. After his teammates Nightcrawler and Kitty Pryde were critically injured, Peter finally snapped, breaking the neck of one of the villainous Marauders.

On a trip to his homeland, Peter's parents were killed and he returned to America with his little sister Illyana (who had once been a member of the NEW MUTANTS when her ageing process had been altered by being in Limbo). Shortly after it was revealed that Illyana had caught the Legacy Virus, which caused a disease lethal to mutants. Professor Xavier and Henry McCoy fought long and hard to save Illyana, but they knew so little about the condition that Peter's 'Little Snowflake' never really stood a chance.

At her funeral, Professor Xavier tried to comfort Peter, but Peter lost his temper, the months of doubt and pain having taken their toll. He blamed Xavier for the deaths and hurting and asked, perhaps understandably, how much more the X-MEN's 'dream' could cost him?

At that moment Magneto attacked the gathered X-MEN, X-FACTOR and X-FORCE. Peter defended the Master of Magnetism and agreed to stay with him, much to the despair of his former comrades.

Xavier defeated Magneto and destroyed the latter's mind in a last-ditch effort to save thousands of lives. Peter refused to return and took Magneto back to his base, Avalon.

While Professor Xavier understood the decision he still believes that his failures were responsible for Peter's choice.

THE 1970s

In many ways, the 1970s proved both the high and low point of X-MEN history.

By the end of the 1960s, Roy Thomas had hired a talented new artist called Neal Adams, whose dramatic style was destined to win a new set of fans. His figures were more dynamic and his panel structure reflected the action in each illustration. But even this was not enough to save the X-MEN from a greater foe — the circulation wars.

From #67 (cover-dated December 1970), the X-MEN comic only published reprint material from the early issues, beginning with the origin of Professor X (originally published in #12). The comic book returned to the original bi-monthly schedule.

Marvel Girl vs Magneto as a new decade dawned.

The problem was that while the X-MEN had a strong following, the comic itself was not blazing its way through Marvel's coffers. The reprints continued to be printed until 1975.

Then something remarkable happened. GIANT-SIZE X-MEN #1 hit the stands and the X-MEN were, literally, never the same again.

In the intervening years, Roy Thomas had gone on to become Marvel's Editor-in-Chief. He vacated that position shortly before the magazine became available to the public, but he was involved in early discussions. He attended a meeting with Stan Lee and Marvel's President Al Landau.

'Al Landau said that if we could come up with a group book that had several characters from several different countries – and of course we would target particular countries – we could sell the book abroad,' remembers Thomas. Thomas's first choice came from his old stompin' ground: THE X-MEN.

Len Wein and Dave Cockrum were selected to write and draw the comic respectively. By the time it hit the stands Wein had also become the book's editor. Though the original idea might have been based around marketing, many characters in the new line-up came from countries where comics were hardly likely to be snapped up (such as the Soviet Union's Colossus and Kenya's Storm). Wein and Cockrum deny ever having been influenced by the marketing origins.

Neil Adams' distinctive style was popular with the fans.

Enter Moira MacTaggert, Housekeeper with attitude.

BIOGRAPHY
CYCLOPS

1st Appearance: X-MEN #1

Scott 'Slim' Summers was the eldest son of Christopher Summers, a Major and test pilot, and Katherine Anne Summers. Returning from vacation the family's private vintage aircraft, carrying Scott, his parents and his brother Alex, encountered an interplanetary Shi'ar scouting craft. The wooden plane burst into flames. Katherine Summers strapped her sons into the one surviving parachute and pushed them to safety. (The brothers believed their parents to be dead until Scott, years later, learned that Christopher had escaped and now led the interstellar STARJAMMERS.)

Scott and Alex were found with serious injuries and amnesia. Alex recovered (physically) first and was sent to an orphanage where he was soon adopted. Scott, however, remained comatose for a year and suffered some minimal brain damage.

Scott was sent to an orphanage in Nebraska. Unfairly considered unsuitable for adoption because of his difficulties, Scott remained there until his mid-teens. Later it was to be revealed that a villainous 'Mr Sinister' had, in fact, deliberately kept Scott there to learn more about him and his possible mutant abilities.

Those abilities manifested themselves shortly after Scott visited New York City (in a bid to find a cure for his headaches and eye-strain). Accidentally, he triggered his eye-blasts, destroying a crane in the middle of the city. Despite his saving onlookers from the falling debris with another blast, the mob turned on him and he became a wanted man. Professor Xavier and a sympathetic FBI agent, Fred Duncan, tracked him down and Xavier recruited Scott to be the founding member of the original X-MEN alongside his current student Jean Grey. Scott, as Cyclops, led the original team and continued to lead it after many of the original members had moved on. Jean Grey left the team, but remained in contact with Scott as their love grew. Jean apparently became the cosmic Phoenix who months later was forced to take her own life in order to save the fabric of the universe. Scott left the team for a while but remained in contact with its members.

On a trip to Alaska, Scott met Madelyne Pryor, a woman who was the spitting image of the 'dead' Jean Grey. After much soul-searching Scott and Maddie married. He formally resigned from the X-MEN and the couple had a son, Nathan Christopher. Shortly afterwards it was revealed that Jean Grey had in fact never been the Phoenix and was alive and well. Scott returned to meet the original X-MEN and formed X-FACTOR. It was later disclosed that Madelyne Pryor was in fact a clone of Jean Grey; she turned against Scott and the X-Teams and was killed in the battle. Scott returned with the original X-FACTOR/X-MEN and led the X-MEN's Blue Team.

Recently (and at long, long last) Jean and Scott were finally married.

MIXED BLESSINGS

BIOGRAPHY
EXCALIBUR

When Kitty Pryde (Shadowcat) and Kurt Wagner (Nightcrawler) were critically injured during the X-MEN's fight with the Marauders, their injuries were so great that much of their treatment and convalescence took place on Muir Island. It was during this time that they learned of their comrades' 'deaths' in a mystical battle with a creature known as the Adversary.

At around the same time, Rachel Summers (the second 'Phoenix') escaped the psychotic, dimensionally-challenged entity known as Mojo.

Brian Braddock (Captain Britain) and his lover Meggan mourned the loss of his sister Betsy (Psylocke) who had recently joined the X-MEN and was then believed to be dead. With a metallic self-aware creation known as 'Widget', these heroes joined together to save Phoenix from Mojo's Warwolves and, as EXCALIBUR, took the place of the X-MEN.

Even when it was revealed that the X-MEN had actually been restored to life and stayed in hiding, Excalibur continued to function from its British base. Later they were joined by the lion-like Feron, Shi'ar rogue Cerise and a new, improved Widget.

Founding Members Bios:

Captain Britain: Brian Braddock, empowered by Merlin to protect the ancient isle. He possesses great strength which is partially channelled through his uniform.

Meggan: A shape-changer whose form reacts to mood and emotions. An innocent still trying to find her way in the world. Totally in love with Brian.

Shadowcat: Kitty Pryde, with the ability to phase through solid objects. Still in her teens, but her extensive time and experiences with the X-MEN have made her wise beyond her years.

Nightcrawler: Kurt Wagner, with the ability to teleport or 'BAMF' from place to place. Also has the ability to vanish into shadows and is a great acrobat... oh, and he's blue and fuzzy! Recently revealed to be Mystique's son.

Phoenix II: Scott Summers and Jean Grey's daughter from an alternate future, with the ability to travel (with limitations) in time. She is also the channel for part of the original Phoenix force.

Lockheed: When Kitty Pryde and the X-MEN faced the alien Brood (see Checklist) they accidentally brought back to Earth a small, purple and incredibly cool dragon. Kitty christened him Lockheed and he's been devoted to her since!

Widget: Originally and inexplicably a small, self-aware metallic entity, Widget has the ability to access other dimensions. On a recent trip to Rachel's future, the life-force of Kate Pryde (an older Kitty) also became part of its makeup. Now in a more humanoid form.

Cerise: Actually on the run from the Shi'ar Empire, it was revealed that she was wanted for war crimes, though under extenuating circumstances. She fought alongside Excalibur and then returned to the Empire to face her accusers.

Kylun: A young mutant who stumbled through a dimensional gate opened by Widget. He grew up to become a fierce warrior with the added mutant ability to replicate any sound. He took time off from the team to locate his parents.

Micromax: Never actually a member, but an ally. A.k.a. Radio DJ Scott Wright. Vain and conceited, he has the ability to alter his size proportionally. Currently pursuing a more 'commercial' career.

Feron: Young mystic whose attitude makes Micromax look well-adjusted. He was brought up to become one with the Phoenix force and was more than a little miffed to find it already in the hands of Rachel Summers.

HISTORY

'The marketing aspect of the business was not on my mind at all. Dave Cockrum and I just looked for an interesting combination – someone from here, someone from there,' admits Wein.

The opening story saw the original X-MEN captured by a 'living island' known as Krakoa. Professor X had no choice but to recruit a new team to rescue them. He selected a team from all over the world. They were:

Ororo Munroe from Kenya	**Storm**
Kurt Wagner from Germany	**Nightcrawler**
John Proudstar, Native American	**Thunderbird**
Peter Rasputin from Russia	**Colossus**
Logan, Canadian	**Wolverine**

All of these were characters new to the Marvel Universe, with the exception of Wolverine who had made his debut in the monthly INCREDIBLE HULK title.

Together with the only free member of the original X-MEN, Cyclops, this 'second genesis' team managed to defeat Krakoa and release the others. At the end of the issue is a historic and climactic question: 'What are we going to do with 13 X-MEN?'

The answer was, in fact, quite simple. In both the story and the comic itself, it was a time for new blood. The original team had grown up and

Chris Claremont with Louise Jone (ex-X-Editor).

Nightcrawler, of the second generation of X-MEN, was originally designed by Dave Cockrum for a team of heroes at DC comics!

Claremont's writing, Byrne's pencils and Terry Asutin's inks combine for an understated effect as Jean tells Xavier of the other X-MEN's 'deaths'.

become adept in the use of their powers. In truth, there was no real reason for them to stay at the school and so, quite simply, they graduated.

The X-MEN are captured and mesmerized into performing as circus acts.

With the exception of Scott Summers (Cyclops), who had grown comfortable in the Mansion, the only real home he'd known, the original X-MEN left the team, although they were later to make appearances in the book (especially Jean Grey who was romantically involved with Scott).

The ongoing story of the 'All-New, All-Different X-MEN' continued in the monthly title #94 and the writing chores were taken over by a man who stayed with the title for over a decade. The writer's name was Chris Claremont.

He was given the job by new Editor-in-Chief Len Wein and quickly established the new team. Within one issue, Thunderbird was killed and Claremont began further to define the characters.

'For the first couple of years, Dave Cockrum and I were making it up as we went along,' said Claremont. 'And our interests meshed.' Wolverine

Moira's son, Proteus, had the power to warp reality and caused a few headaches for the X-MEN.

was revealed to be older than first envisioned and the writers gave Nightcrawler a much lighter personality, believing that being blue and fuzzy could be quite cool.

'The trick with X-MEN was that you couldn't read just one issue. Something about it would be so interesting that you'd want to come back for the next one,' explained Claremont. Though it would still be a few years before the X-MEN became the phenomenon they are today, here were the first strands of the plots that would eventually take the series there.

Cockrum left the comic in October 1977, but not before illustrating such stories as the X-MEN's clash with the new Sentinels and the rise of the entity known as the Phoenix. The next issue saw an artist who would become as big a

When Proteus unnerves the team, Cyclops improvises a solution.

1st Appearance: UNCANNY X-MEN #266

BIOGRAPHY

GAMBIT

Remy LeBeau deliberately keeps his past shrouded in mystery. The Cajun adventurer hails from New Orleans where he was a member of the ancient Thieves Guild and a reluctant player in the subsequent war of the clans.

Betrothed to Belladonna, of the rival Assassins Guild, he fled the arranged marriage and fuelled the clan rivalry.

LeBeau met up with the X-MAN Storm when she found herself in the body of a young child and for a time they 'worked' the streets of New Orleans as thieves. Gambit helped Storm escape the clutches of the Shadow King, a villainous telepath, and went with Storm when she returned to the X-MEN. For a while he stayed on the edge of the team, more a guest than a member of the X-MEN.

Gradually, through various battles, he became a mainstream member of the X-MEN. His ability to 'charge' small objects with energy and use them as missiles proved invaluable on numerous occasions. He has become very close to Rogue, but due to her power-absorbing abilities the romance has had to move slowly.

The relationship was further complicated by the appearance of LeBeau's wife Belladonna, who requested the help of the X-MEN in defeating the alien Brood. In the ensuing battle Belladonna was apparently killed, though a few months later it appeared she had somehow survived.

For all his heroism, there are many who question the trust they have placed in him. Past associates and enemies have commented that Gambit is not as trustworthy as he appears to be and that a sinister motive lies behind the happy-go-lucky facade. Bishop still believes that Gambit could betray the team. One thing is certain, Gambit has more than a few skeletons in his past, none of which he is anxious to share.

Whether his future lies as enemy or friend, only time will tell. For the moment he functions as a valued member of the X-MEN's Blue Team.

contributor to the team's success as Claremont. His name was John Byrne.

For the next four years Claremont and Byrne carefully wrote, drew and soon co-plotted the adventures of the team that was rapidly becoming Marvel's best-selling comic book. More than ever, the X-MEN were presented as real people and as much attention was paid to their personal lives as to their costumed escapades.

In the months that followed the X-MEN saved the universe and travelled the globe. Alpha Flight was introduced as the Canadian outfit that Wolverine had belonged to before quitting to join the X-MEN. Claremont and Byrne also continued to give the team well-rounded personalities by throwing them into situations that would test different parts of their characters.

Weapon Alpha (Vindicator) vs Weapon X (Wolverine).

Hot on Vindicator's heels, the other members of Alpha Flight are soon ordered to track down Wolverine.

The title of the story is cleverly embodied in the frame and mood of this splash page from X-MEN #114.

A typically busy scene from John Byrne... but hold on, who invited the phantom stranger and Popeye ???

Scott and Jean get mushy...

In #113 the X-MEN took on the might of Magneto. The final scenes show Phoenix and Beast separated from the rest of the team as Magneto's Antarctic base is destroyed. Over the next year, the readers of the comic book followed the X-MEN as they journeyed to the Savage Land and Japan and also watched Phoenix and Beast begin to re-build their lives. Each team believed the other to have perished in their fight with Magneto. The combination of tight writing and emotive panels showed how each member coped with the tragedy.

But even before reuniting the X-MEN, Byrne and Claremont were sowing the seeds of a story that would round off the '70s and begin the '80s with one of the most talked-about epics in not only the X-MEN's history but that of the whole Marvel Universe.

THE 1980S

If there was any doubt that the X-MEN were the most popular team in comics, the early 1980s showed exactly why they had got there in the first place.

The X-MEN began to investigate the dealings of an organisation that readers had glimpsed only in shadows. They were the Hellfire Club (incidentally based on a real 18th-century secret society infamous for its debauchery). In the process, we were introduced to Dazzler, a disco-diva mutant complete with roller-skates and flares (thankfully taken a little more seriously later) and a

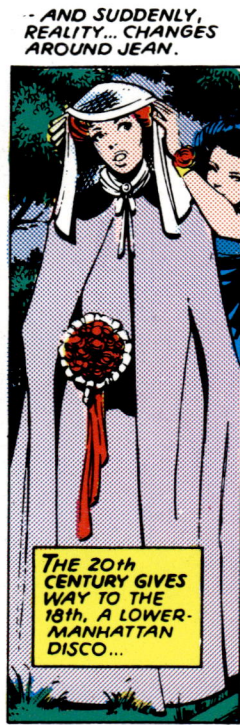

Jason Wyngarde manipulates Jean Grey...

THE ESSENTIAL GUIDE

WILT THOU, JASON, HAVE THIS WOMAN TO BE THY WEDDED WIFE? WILT THOU LOVE HER, COMFORT HER, HONOR AND KEEP HER IN SICKNESS AND IN HEALTH AND, FORSAKING ALL OTHERS, KEEP THEE ONLY UNTO HER, SO LONG AS YE BOTH SHALL LIVE?

I WILL.

WILT THOU, LADY JEAN, HAVE THIS MAN...?

Oh, YES! YES!!

Smiling, his obsidian eyes glowing with an eerie, darkling light, the minister finishes the ceremony...

...I PRONOUNCE THAT THEY BE MAN AND WIFE! SIR, YOU MAY KISS THE BRIDE.

YOU'RE MINE NOW, MILADY. BOUND TO ME TILL THE END OF TIME!

MILORD, I WOULD NOT HAVE IT ANY OTHER WAY!

MILORDS, GENTLEMEN -- LADIES -- OF THE HELLFIRE CLUB-- I GIVE YOU JEAN GREY, OUR **BLACK QUEEN**!

"LONG MAY SHE REIGN!!"

The ruined, desecrated churchyard explodes with cheers, but Jean hears none of them...

...as every facet of her being is overwhelmed by a physical and emotional tidal wave, the like of which she has never known.

...creating a Dark Queen who's going to become much darker...

Then, as abruptly as it began, the timeslip ends...

≧!?!≦ ≧?!?≦

> AND SO, A REAL QUICK CHANGE, AN EIGHT-BLOCK **[**CREAM SODA LATER, A KID FROM MIDDLE AMERICA **[**TO BECOMING FAST FRIENDS.

"WE GOT BLACK KIDS IN MY SCHOOL, ORORO, BUT NONE OF 'EM LOOK LIKE YOU. I MEAN, Y'KNOW-- WHITE HAIR AN' BLUE EYES??"

"YOU MEAN, 'CAUSE I'M SO SMART?"

youthful Kitty Pryde, a teenage mutant with the ability to phase through solid objects.

Emma Frost (the Hellfire Club's White Queen) tried to persuade Kitty to join her school just as Xavier had persuaded her to join the X-MEN, though her secret goals were obviously less scrupulous. The X-MEN realised that they now had direct opposition not only on a battle level but on an educational level.

> ...LK AND A TRIPLE-SCOOP, "SOOPER-DOOPER" ICE
> ...D AN AFRICAN "GODDESS" ARE WELL ON THE WAY

> SO FAR AS I KNOW, KITTY, I AM ONE OF A KIND. AND SO ARE YOU.

> NO-- SOMETHING ELSE. KITTY, HAVE YOU EVER HEARD OF THE X-MEN?

Kitty and Ororo strike up their life-long friendship.

Jason Wyngarde, actually the X-MEN's old foe Mastermind, delighted in playing mind-games with Jean Grey, not fully comprehending the power he was dealing with. He managed to corrupt Jean and the X-MEN, minus Wolverine, were captured. It was only through her love for Scott and the actions of Wolverine that the tide turned in the X-MEN's favour. The battle had been won, but a savage new enemy had been unleashed. Phoenix, a being of cosmic

HISTORY

Too late... the pieces fall into place...

Uh-oh -- Wyngarde's taking Jean upstairs.

Jean?! Wait up-- Jean!

She's ignoring me! What kind of hold does Wyngarde have over her?!

How charming -- the stalwart hero out to rescue his damsel fair.

Not this time, Cyclops!

Wha--?! That FACE!

MASTERMIND!

The night the X-Men met Dazzler, Scott saw Jason Wyngarde momentarily silhouetted in the headlights of the X-Men's Rolls-Royce...

...throwing a shadow on the wall behind him that didn't match his face. Scott should have RECOGNIZED the master of illusion.*

But he was in a hurry, with far more immediate worries on his mind. And so, he made a mistake.

I'd better get to Jean fast! If she's under Mastermind's influence...

*IN CLASSIC X-MEN #36, PAGE 17, PANEL 3 -- BAFFLED BOB.

Too late, Cyclops!

AARRRGH!

SPLOW!

Magnificent, my love.

But-- the Hellfire Club wants the X-Men alive. Is Cyclops--?

Worry not, Jason.

Had the BLACK QUEEN struck to kill, there would be nothing left of the lad but ASHES.

powers, had been almost totally corrupted and driven insane. While Phoenix had the power to save the universe, Dark Phoenix had the power to destroy it. The X-MEN didn't stand a chance.

Dark Phoenix destroyed a faraway inhabited star system (inhabited by 'asparagus people', as Byrne and Claremont called them). Then she returned to kill the X-MEN. The team was torn. They had virtually no hope of surviving an encounter with Dark Phoenix and none wanted to fight his teammate. It finally came down to a battle of wills between Xavier and Dark Phoenix. Xavier managed to shut some of Phoenix's psychic 'doors' and Phoenix appeared to lose her power, reverting to the power level and purity of Jean Grey. But Dark Phoenix had destroyed a Shi'ar starship and her crew and the Shi'ar Empire demanded her execution. The X-MEN had to fight for the life of their team-mate.

Mastermind unwittingly unleashes ultimate power.

The original outcome for the life-battle saw the X-MEN defeated and Phoenix drained of her powers, becoming in some ways a shadow of her former fiery self. She and Scott were to leave the X-MEN and begin their lives anew.

HISTORY

That was the original intention. It didn't quite happen that way...

By now Jim Shooter was Editor-in-Chief at Marvel. One of his jobs was to read the various mock-up issues before they went off to print. He read #137 – Fate of the Phoenix – and wasn't happy. Phoenix, insane or not, had killed a whole planet-load of asparagus people and the crew of a starship. In short she had committed wilful murder and in Shooter's eyes she was getting away with it. If 'Jean Grey' survived, powers or not, the comic book would seem to be minimising the significance of a crime on that scale. He decided, not without strong opposition, that 'Jean' could not survive the battle for her life on the Moon.

The calm before the storm...

At the end of #137, 'Jean' feels the Phoenix force returning. Xavier has only delayed the inevitable. In one last heroic act of will, Phoenix says farewell to Scott and kills herself to save the universe.

The next issue, due to begin with a peaceful garden scene featuring Jean and Scott, instead began at the graveside of 'Jean Grey' with a recap of the X-MEN's time together. It also re-introduced Kitty Pryde as Xavier's new pupil.

The death of Jean Grey and the subsequent reactions of her team-mates continued to be visually and narratively dramatic. It seemed that the team had been through every possible dramatic and tragic situation they could. But Claremont and Byrne weren't resting on their laurels and a few issues later saw a two-part story that ranks with the Phoenix saga as one of the most classic stories in the history of the comic.

Wolvie on the prowl in the Hellfire Club.

BIOGRAPHY
ICEMAN

1st Appearance: X-MEN #1

⊗ ICEMAN

Robert 'Bobby' Drake was born with the mutant ability to generate extreme cold and freeze the very moisture in the air. His parents, aware of the implications of their son's power and the reactions it might provoke, insisted that Bobby keep his abilities a secret. This was possible until one evening, on a date with his girlfriend, Bobby was forced to 'freeze' a local bully who attacked them.

News soon spread and a lynch mob of the townsfolk went looking for him. Bobby was arrested and taken to the local police station, mainly for his own protection.

Professor Xavier learned of the incident and sent Cyclops (Scott Summers) to free the young mutant. Bobby refused to go with Cyclops and the resulting fight nearly led to both mutants being hanged by the frightened townsfolk. Professor Xavier intervened, mentally calming the town and erasing details from their collective memory. Bobby's parents consented to allow Bobby to become a pupil at Xavier's School for Gifted Youngsters and Bobby became a founding member of the original X-MEN.

After graduating from the team, Bobby went on to join two other teams alongside the Beast, both of which disbanded after a short time. Bobby returned to his studies, but kept contacts with his former team-mates.

When Warren Worthington brought the original members of the X-MEN back together, Bobby became a member of the first X-FACTOR. The ex-X-MEN returned to Xavier's mansion and Bobby became a member of its Gold Team.

Bobby often feels that he is treated as a 'second-string' player and that he doesn't get the respect that his team-mates enjoy. However he has constantly proved himself in battle and now has even greater control of his mutant abilities.

In #141 and #142 writer Chris Claremont and artist John Byrne created a time-travel tale that brought the X-MEN's purpose bang into focus. Days Of Future Past began in the 21st century and showed how America had become controlled by Sentinels. Almost every super-being had been wiped out or captured. Mutants were kept in concentration camps, forced to wear the letter M, a futuristic 'scarlet letter'.

Scott reaches out to Dark Phoenix.

Wolverine, Magneto, Kate Pryde (an older and wiser Kitty), Storm, Colossus, Franklin Richards and Rachel Summers hatch a plan to break out of one of the maximum security camps and send Kate's psyche back to the mind of 20th-century Kitty. She must convince the X-MEN of our day that the assassination of Senator Robert Kelly will lead to this desolate future and help prevent the tragedy from ever occurring.

In the 21st century, the others try to protect Kate's physical body. Slowly, one by one, each X-Man is killed by the Sentinels until only Rachel remains. Kitty/Kate succeeds in her mission, but her future time-line seems to be unaffected.

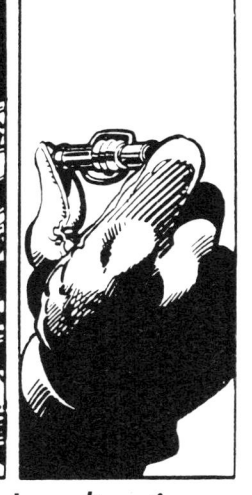

This story reflected the darker, grittier approach that had been developing over the years. Strongly illustrated and written, the plot led the reader into the very nightmare the X-MEN had been pledged to prevent. We are given glimpses of characters that we know and love, only to see them die, heroes to the last. While Kate is successful, we are left wondering if this one alteration will actually prevent a similar set of fates in the future.

A few issues later, John Byrne left the X-MEN to pursue other projects and Dave Cockrum returned to illustrate the title.

One of the hardest-hitting X-MEN stories ever to see print didn't actually appear in the main monthly title. In 1982 Marvel published a graphic novel

In an alternative future an older 'Kate' Pryde and Wolverine plan an escape.

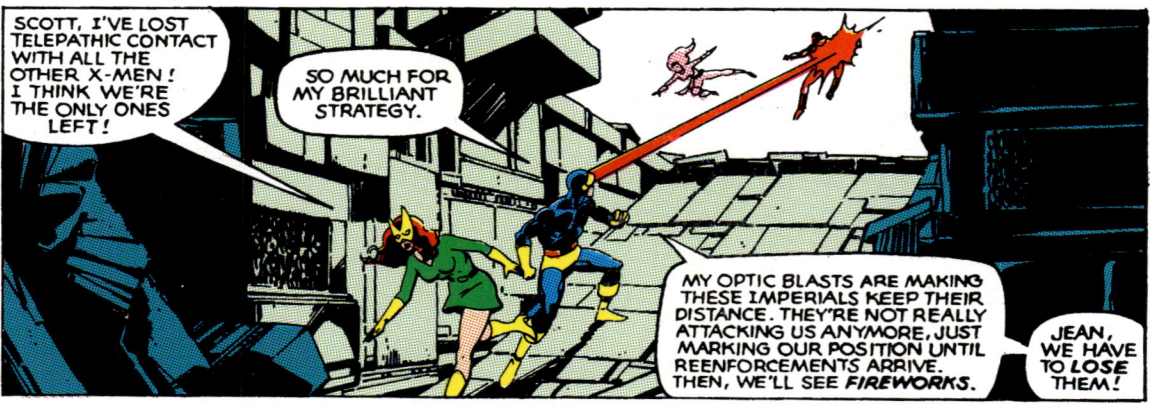

The X-MEN fight for Jean's life on the moon.

BIOGRAPHY

JEAN GREY
MARVEL GIRL

1st Appearance: X-MEN #1

At the age of ten, Jean Grey witnessed her best friend, Annie Richardson, being knocked down by a speeding car. Annie died in Jean's arms, but as she did so Jean was flooded with the girl's feelings and pain. Depressed and traumatised by the incident, which was a result of her awakening telepathic abilities, Jean was sent to Professor Xavier for treatment. Xavier helped Jean to come to terms with these new sensations. Shortly afterwards, Xavier began recruiting the members of the first X-MEN and Jean became the fifth member.

For years the team fought together until they were captured and Xavier recruited a new team to rescue them. The original X-MEN decided that the time had come to graduate and leave the team. Only Scott Summers decided to stay at the mansion. Jean had fallen in love with Scott, but decided she had to leave to find herself.

She did, however, remain in close contact with the team. Jean and the X-MEN were kidnapped by a madman named Steven Lang and his Sentinels. They were taken aboard his space-station where they finally defeated him. However, they still had to return to Earth and with solar flares in full fury, death seemed almost certain. Willing to sacrifice herself for the team and the man she loved, Jean took control of the returning space shuttle and tried to steer the craft home, all the while using her telekinetic abilities to hold back the radiation. In the final moments the shield failed and the shuttle crashed back to Earth.

The X-MEN survived but Jean seemed changed, her powers amplified to a huge degree, and she became known as the 'Phoenix'. Over the next few months, Xavier became concerned with her boosted powers, realising that 'power corrupts and absolute power corrupts absolutely'. Eventually he was proved right as a 'Dark' Phoenix surfaced and went on the rampage. Xavier briefly cured Jean of the effects of her power, but she was made to stand trial for the destruction of a whole planet ! The X-MEN were forced to defend her on Earth's Moon, but as Dark Phoenix began to resurface, she realised what would happen and took her own life to save her friends and the universe itself.

Scott mourned her and left the X-MEN. Years later, a cocoon was found deep at sea. With the help of the Fantastic Four, the cocoon was opened. Inside was Jean Grey. She had, in fact, never been Phoenix. Phoenix was a cosmic entity that had taken her form and cocooned the dying Jean Grey until she had recovered from the radiation.

Scott, recently married, returned to meet her and together they joined the first X-FACTOR. Scott's wife, Maddie, was later revealed as a clone of Jean and eventually turned against the teams. Maddie was killed and Scott and Jean cared for Scott's son Nathan Christopher, who was later sent to the future in hope of finding a cure for Apocalypse's techno-infection.

Jean and Scott returned to the X-MEN and recently, at long last, married.

called 'God Loves, Man Kills'. If there was ever a story that showed why the X-MEN were formed and what they continued to fight for, this was it.

Presented with maturity and with little compromise, 'God Loves, Man Kills' tells the story of Reverend Stryker, a right-wing anti-mutant evangelist who sees all mutants as '...abominations in the sight of the Lord'. The Reverend is charismatic and in many ways an honourable man. He is not some super-villain out to conquer the world; he is a man who passionately believes in his own interpretation of the Bible and his faith. In his own eyes he is simply campaigning for what he believes to be a noble ideal. But he is also a man who believes that the end justifies the means. The opening pages of the graphic novel show the fate of two young children, lynched simply because they are mutants. It is a harrowing beginning which sets the tone for this more morally ambiguous version of the X-MEN's world.

The X-MEN and Magneto are drawn into the story as Stryker's campaign becomes more and more high profile and the attacks on mutants more and more frequent. The final confrontation takes place at a rally in a huge stadium in front of thousands of eyes and cameras. The sub-plots also hit home, and just as hard. Stevie Hunter (Kitty Pryde's black dance tutor and confidant of the mutant team) tells the young X-Man to ignore the ramblings of a bully-boy pupil who's spouted off about Kitty being a 'mutie-lover'. After all, she explains, they are only words. Kitty turns on Stevie and asks her if she '... would be so damned tolerant if he'd called me a nigger-lover'. Harsh and controversial words for any comic book — yet we suddenly see very clearly what it must be like to be a young mutant in the Marvel Universe and how easy it is to forget how unthinking people can be. It is Chris Claremont's writing and Brent Anderson's illustrations at their best and will silence anybody who would tell you that comics are only for kids.

In this alternative future most of the X-MEN are dead.

Through the '80s, the X-MEN were drawn by some of the hottest artists in the business including Paul Smith (an ex-animator) and Mark Silvestri. The team ventured into space and were infected by the Brood. Only Wolverine fought off

The cover for X-MEN #141

the alien egg effects. He swore to kill the X-MEN rather than see them turned into the vicious Brood. In the end it didn't come to that but the space saga continued to highlight ways that the X-MEN reacted to different situations. Marvel also introduced Xavier's newest pupils, aptly called the NEW MUTANTS.

Rogue, a former member of the Brotherhood of Evil Mutants and foster-daughter of the shape-shifting Mystique, joined the team when she searched out

HISTORY

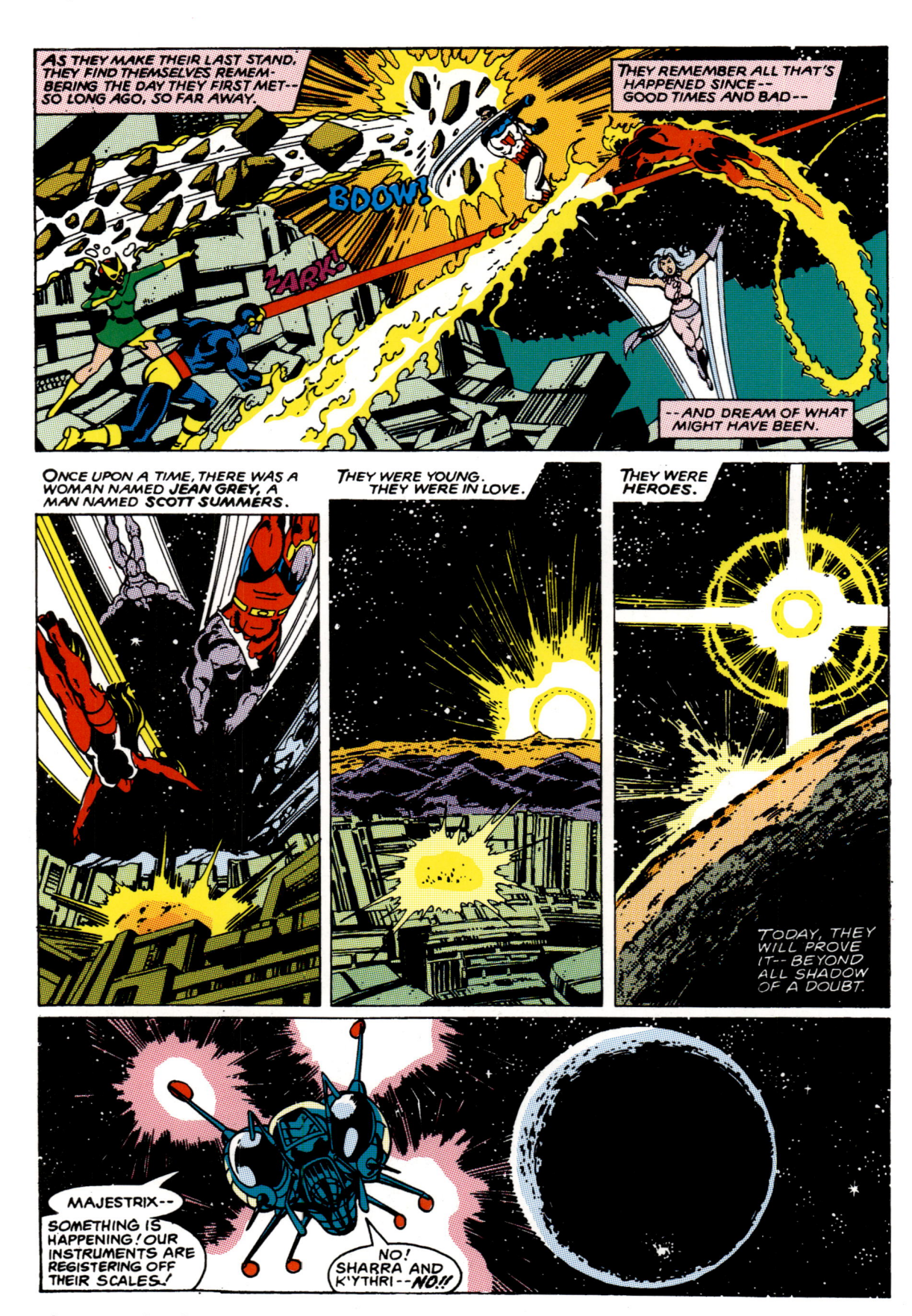

AS THEY MAKE THEIR LAST STAND, THEY FIND THEMSELVES REMEMBERING THE DAY THEY FIRST MET-- SO LONG AGO, SO FAR AWAY.

THEY REMEMBER ALL THAT'S HAPPENED SINCE-- GOOD TIMES AND BAD--

--AND DREAM OF WHAT MIGHT HAVE BEEN.

ONCE UPON A TIME, THERE WAS A WOMAN NAMED **JEAN GREY**, A MAN NAMED **SCOTT SUMMERS**.

THEY WERE YOUNG. THEY WERE IN LOVE.

THEY WERE HEROES.

TODAY, THEY WILL PROVE IT-- BEYOND ALL SHADOW OF A DOUBT.

MAJESTRIX-- SOMETHING IS HAPPENING! OUR INSTRUMENTS ARE REGISTERING OFF THEIR SCALES!

NO! SHARRA AND K'YTHRI-- *NO!!*

...but it's too late for Jean...

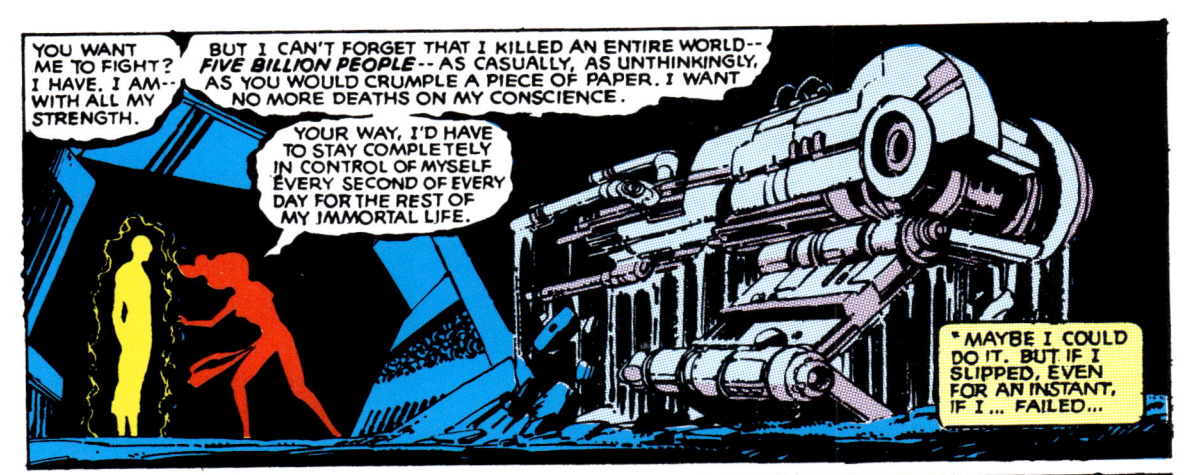

...far too late...

HISTORY

Professor Xavier to help her deal with her psi-problems (as a result of absorbing Ms Marvel's whole psyche). The X-MEN were dubious of Xavier's decision to enrol her at the school, but she became a firm member of the team. 1983 also saw Logan (Wolverine) betrothed to Mariko Yashida and we saw a gentler side of the savage warrior. The wedding didn't happen due to the manipulations of an old X-MEN villain, Mastermind. Storm also changed radically with a new punk look. Needless to say it raised a few eyebrows. At the same time Scott came face to face with a woman who was the mirror image of Jean Grey who called herself Madelyne Pryor. The ramifications of that meeting would eventually shake the X-MEN's world apart.

Rachel (Scott and Jean's future daughter, last seen in 'The Days Of Future Past') travelled down-time and joined up with the X-MEN. In 1985 Rachel took on the mantle of her late mother and became Phoenix.

Disillusioned with his war against humanity, Magneto agreed to face his accusers and stood trial for his past crimes. Xavier, his body pushed to its limits, was gravely injured in an attack and Magneto agreed to take over as tutor to the New Mutants.

In 1986, a cocooned body was found deep on the ocean floor. Inside was the restored body of... Jean Grey. The being that the team had known as Phoenix was a cosmic entity that had taken Jean's form when she nearly died saving the X-MEN as they returned to Earth after fighting Lang's Sentinels. Phoenix had cocooned Jean's body until it had recovered. It had taken on the vestiges of humanity and managed eventually to save the universe by using Jean's better qualities as an anchor to hold on as long as she did. By this time Scott had married Madelyne and had a son, Nathan Christopher. Scott returned to face Jean and the old X-MEN formed X-FACTOR. Madelyne and the baby disappeared without trace.

Also in 1986, The X-MEN faced the merciless Marauders, a team of mercenary mutants working for the mysterious Mr Sinister, and who were now slaughtering the Morlocks who lived below New York. Shadowcat (Kitty Pryde), Nightcrawler (Kurt Wagner) and Colossus were gravely injured and effectively had to withdraw from active status. In the months that followed the X-MEN welcomed new recruits Longshot, Dazzler and Scott's younger brother Alex (Havok). Once they had recovered, Shadowcat and Nightcrawler joined a new British superhero team, EXCALIBUR, created by Claremont and British artist Alan Davis.

By 1988 readers were beginning to see that there was more to Madelyne Pryor than her looks. It was revealed that she was in fact a clone of Jean Grey, created by a being called Mr Sinister. She had been awakened by the death of 'Jean' on the Moon. Sinister had planned to mate Pryor and Summers to create powerful mutant DNA.

With Jean back he had tried to kill Pryor but she had survived. For a time Madelyne sought sanctuary from the Marauders and when the X-MEN sacrificed their lives to stop the mystical entity known as the Adversary, she joined them.

Roma, guardian of the multiverse, restored the group to life and for a while the X-MEN operated from a secret base in Australia, hitting back at enemies who believed them to be dead. Perhaps Madelyne had never actually known the truth about her origins but the hate she felt over what she regarded as Scott's betrayal of their love pushed her over the edge. She became the Goblin Queen and the X-MEN were forced to fight her to the death.

It was another death for the X-MEN to face, another hurt to recover from...and fans loved every minute as the title stayed firmly at the top of the comic charts. By the end of the '80s Claremont and Silvestri co-created a popular new member for the X-MEN, the teenage Asian-American girl, Jubilee.

Marvel experimented with increasing the publication count per year. During the summer months of the late '80s, Marvel published two issues of the title per month. This also led to more sales. Several spin-off series featuring the X-MEN characters also achieved great success, including THE NEW MUTANTS, X-FACTOR, WOLVERINE and EXCALIBUR.

So the '80s were a drama-packed decade full of trials and tribulations, but as one decade ended a new chapter was about to start for the X-MEN...

John Byrne

WHAT THE HELL IS GOING ON OUT HERE!?!

IT'S KITTY'S FAULT, MS. HUNTER! SHE STARTED IT!

IS THIS TRUE?

I SWUNG FIRST--

--BECAUSE DANNY SHOT HIS MOUTH OFF ONCE TOO OFTEN!

YOUR TURN, DANIEL. EXPLAIN.

I WAS TALKIN' ABOUT THE STRYKER CRUSADE, AN' ALL THE GOOD IT DOES.

MY FOLKS AN' I ARE MEMBERS, WHAT'S WRONG WITH THAT?

TELL HER THE REST, CREEP-- ABOUT HOW REVEREND STRYKER'S GONNA SAVE HUMANITY...

...FROM THE GODLESS HORDES OF **MUTANTKIND!**

WELL, HE IS! MUTIES ARE EVIL! THEY DESERVE WHATEVER THEY GET!

YOU WANNA MAKE SOMETHIN' OF IT, MUTIE-LOVER?!

YOU HAVE BOTH MADE YOUR POINTS, YOUNG MAN. I SUGGEST YOU LET MATTERS END THERE.

RIGHT. HEY, ANYTHING YOU SAY, MR. RASPUTIN. NO PROBLEM.

NEXT TIME, PRYDE--WHEN "KING KONG" HERE ISN'T AROUND TO PROTECT YOU-- IT'LL BE **MY** TURN.

THANKS A LOT, PETER.

FORGIVE ME, KATYA. I SIMPLY DID NOT WANT TO SEE THE BOY HURT.

WITH YOUR TRAINING, YOU COULD'VE CRIPPLED DANNY-- OR WORSE.

HE'D'VE DONE THE SAME TO ME, I BET.

C'MON, LET'S GET YOU INSIDE AND CLEANED UP.

HOW CAN YOU ALL BE SO **CALM**?! DIDN'T YOU HEAR WHAT HE SAID?!

THEY'RE ONLY WORDS, CHILD.

SUPPOSE HE'D CALLED ME A **NIGGER**-LOVER, STEVIE?! WOULD YOU BE SO DAMN' TOLERANT THEN?!!

Without the 'labels', the Marvel universe is pretty close to our own...

1st Appearance: UNCANNY X-MEN #244

BIOGRAPHY

JUBILEE

Jubilation Lee, a mutant human of Asian-American descent, was an orphaned mall-rat living in, around and under a California shopping centre. She had learned to avoid capture by controlling her mutant ability to throw small balls of bright light and concussive force at any pursuers. When Storm, Psylocke and Dazzler teleported into the centre, they piqued the young girl's interest with an unexpected display of powers proving they were mutants like herself. When the X-MEN made a hurried departure, Jubilee hitched a ride back to the X-MEN base in Australia. For several weeks she hid herself away in the complex and no one seemed to be aware of her presence.

When the dispirited X-MEN used a device called the Siege Perilous to leave their 'old' lives, she watched them go and then saw the returning X-MAN, Wolverine, captured by Donald Pierce and his cyborg Reavers. They crucified Wolverine on a huge cross, yet he survived. With his healing factor barely coping, he relied on Jubilee in the days that followed their escape from the complex.

Jubilee and Wolverine then began to track down the missing X-MEN, one by one.

Jubilee stayed with the team more for Wolverine's company than from any desire to be an X-MAN. Despite this attitude and her young age, she rapidly became a valuable, although perhaps the most indiscreet, part of the team. Wolverine was always aware of the debt he owed her and despite his own lack of patience, he made time to look after her.

When Wolverine left the X-MEN after their battle with Magneto, he left her a note saying as much and entrusting her to the care of Professor Xavier.

Jubilee is currently the youngest X-MAN, serving as a member of the Blue Team. She is, therefore, tutored as part of her education at the school (unlike her older team-mates). Naturally, she considers this way, way, way uncool!

THE 1990s

Jim Lee was fast becoming a fan favourite within the industry, particularly with his work on Marvel's PUNISHER. After guesting as penciller on the UNCANNY X-MEN (in which Wolverine and Jubilee search for the missing X-MEN and Psylocke does 'Ninja') it quickly became clear that his dynamic style would be well suited to the top title. Marvel already had plans to expand the range of X-Titles and Jim Lee would be heavily involved. Claremont and Lee co-created a popular new member for the X-MEN, the Cajun mutant, Gambit.

The launch of the X-MEN title (rather than its long established sister THE UNCANNY X-MEN) achieved record sales when it was published in 1990. Several editions of the magazine were published, each cover showing a portion of an enormous picture of the current X-MEN. The X-MEN squared off against Magneto in what seemed to be a final conflict. If it wasn't a swansong for the Master of Magnetism, it was for the long established writer of the X-MEN.

Chris Claremont, who had guided the various titles for longer than many fans had been collecting, decided the time had come for him to leave the title. No one was quite sure what would happen next . But that had always been one of the strengths of the X-Titles: that slight uneasiness caused by the knowledge that things could change very quickly. And, in fact, the X-MEN have continued to remain strong under new writers Fabian Nieiezd (the new X-MEN series and the new mutant comic X-FORCE) and Scott Cobdell (on UNCANNY and the forthcoming GENERATION X).

As the world entered the '90s there was a delicate balance between optimistic steps forward and cynical moves backwards. This was reflected in the stories that surrounded and involved the X-MEN. Some old rivalries and feuds were ended once and for all, while newer and infinitely more dangerous obstacles took their place. More than any other point in the X-MEN history, the fragile line between right and wrong and the principle that the end does not justify the means became less and less clear. Few villains appeared to be settling for all-out battle; more were carefully planning long-running tactics and campaigns. Many, it could be argued, had justifiable reasons for their actions and believed in their causes as strongly as the X-MEN believe in their own. As they did so, the X-MEN were driven to more and more questions on the nature of their role and the price each of them was willing to pay to keep the dream alive.

The '90s have also seen the emergence of a threat, not only to the X-Teams but to every mutant on the planet. Stryfe, Cable's clone, unleashed a terrifying disease known as the Legacy Virus. At the present time it seems to affect only the mutant population. It is a devastating disease that robs mutants of their strength, their will and finally their lives. It appears to be indiscriminate within the mutant community with no single known means of

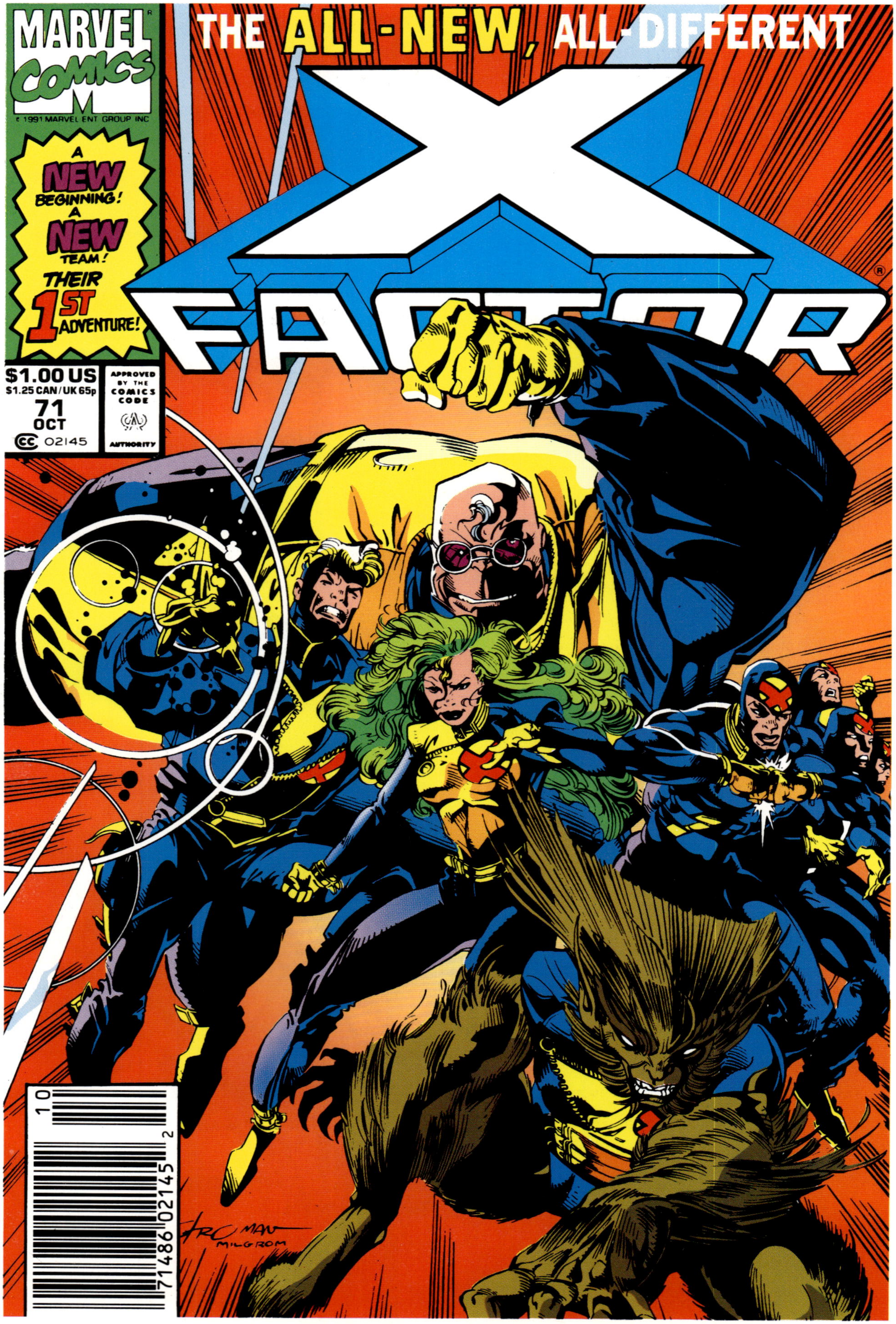

The 'New' X-FACTOR.

contamination and even those at the forefront of biological and genetic science (such as Henry McCoy, Moira MacTaggert and Charles Xavier) have had little success in finding ways to combat the virus. Already it has claimed the lives of Illyana Rasputin, Mastermind and thousands of mutants in Genosha, and many have shown signs of its effects.

More outward threats have included the re-emergence of the Hellfire Club's next generation, the savage Sabretooth's arrival at the mansion and the continuing growth of anti-mutant outbursts.

The team have had the toughest of times: Wolverine critically injured and robbed of his adamantium by Magneto, Peter Rasputin's anguish at the death of his 'little snowflake' Illyana – devastating blows for any time or anyone.

So... who's the future traitor???

But there have also been times of happiness, not least the wedding of Scott and Jean, an event some fans have waited decades to see.

The '90s, like the decades before them, have been a mixed bag of events, triumphs, tragedies and hope for the team and will probably continue to be so well into the next century.

Already plans are laid for GENERATION X, a totally new team that will return to the educational basis of teams like the early X-MEN and the NEW MUTANTS.

HISTORY

This new school will probably have its main base at the Massachusetts Academy, previously run by the Hellfire Club's White Queen Emma Frost and now bought by Xavier. With the Professor's own hands full, its prospective head is Sean Cassidy (Banshee). Whether GENERATION X will reach the heights of the X-MEN only time will tell but with such a rich history to build on, all the X-Teams look set for an interesting future.

Recently launched comics detailing the heroes of the Marvel Universe in 2099 AD show a whole new group of X-MEN, mutants who are still oppressed by society but have banded together to carry on Charles Xavier's dream of peaceful coexistence between mutants and other human beings. But little is known on the fate of their 20th century equivalents... again, only time will tell..!

CANNY...

MARVEL COMICS

X-MEN

$1.25 US
$1.60 CAN/UK 85p
28 JAN

Andy Kubert
matthew ryan

... or UNCANNY, the '90s provide a choice!

THE UNCANNY X-MEN

MARVEL COMICS

$1.25 US
$1.60 CAN
309
FEB
UK 95p

APPROVED BY THE COMICS CODE AUTHORITY

A SECRET CHAPTER OF PROFESSOR XAVIER'S LIFE!

IN MEMORY MOST BITTER!

DIRECT EDITION

Biography X-Men Checklist

Over the years there have been many X-MEN. The bios in this book cover the most recent membership, but who else served time with the team?

Presenting......... the Ex-X-MEN!

THE MIMIC
1st Appearance X-MEN (first series) #19
Calvin Rankin, who was endowed by his scientist father with the ability to mimic the superhuman powers of anyone in his vicinity. Originally an adversary of the X-MEN, he briefly became the team's leader before temporarily losing his powers.

THE CHANGELING
1st Appearance X-MEN (first series) #35
An ex-member of the evil Factor Three, the Changeling learnt he had a terminal illness and tried to redeem himself. As a favour to Prof. Xavier, Changeling impersonated him whilst Xavier was away in deep meditation. He was killed in Xavier's place by a villan called Grotesk.

HAVOK
1st Appearance X-MEN (first series) #54
Alex Summers (Scott's younger brother. See X-FACTOR II entry.

POLARIS
1st Appearance X-MEN (first series) #49
Lorna Dane. See X-FACTOR II entry.

BANSHEE
1st Appearance X-MEN (first series) #28
Sean Cassidy, ex-Interpol Agent, has mutant ability to project intense sonic vibrations vocally. Moira MacTaggert's partner. Usual resident of Muir Island but will soon be relocating to the United States to head new team, GENERATION X.

THUNDERBIRD
1st Appearance GIANT SIZE X-MEN #1
John Proudstar, proud Apache warrior. Killed in action against Count Nefaria. His brother James inherited the name and, as Warpath, is now a member of X-FORCE.

NIGHTCRAWLER
1st Appearance GIANT SIZE X-MEN #1
Blue, furry, elf-like Kurt Wagner saved from an angry German mob by Prof. Xavier. See EXCALIBUR entry.

SUNFIRE
1st Appearance X-MEN (first series) #64
Shiro Yoshida, Japanese warrior, briefly joined the team to help the second generation X-MEN free the original team from Krakoa. Quit immediately afterwards. Currently in Japan.

SHADOWCAT
1st Appearance UNCANNY X-MEN #129
Kitty Pryde, with the ability to phase. Also operated under codenames Sprite and Ariel, both of which she hated. See EXCALIBUR.

DAZZLER
1st Appearance UNCANNY X-MEN #130
Alison Blaire, originally the Disco Dazzler and pop queen, has the ability to generate light-blasts from sufficient sound sources. Currently with Longshot on Mojoworld, where she is expecting their first child.

PHOENIX II
1st Appearance UNCANNY X-MEN #141
Rachel Summers, from an alternate future history. Scott and Jean Summers' daughter in that time-line. See EXCALIBUR entry.

FORGE
1st Appearance UNCANNY X-MEN #184
Mutant inventor who built the weapon that originally robbed Storm of her powers. Currently Government Liaison for X-FACTOR. See X-FACTOR entry.

LONGSHOT
1st Appearance LONGSHOT LIMITED SERIES #1
A fugitive from Mojoworld, a TV-obsessed dimension. He is an artificially created humanoid with the mutant power of incredible luck. Currently back on Mojoworld with Alison Blaire. See DAZZLER entry.

INKERS AND ARTISTS

Over the X-MEN's first thirty or so years there have been many artists with equally different artistic styles. Below is a brief list of the inkers and artists, who enjoyed long and/or significant careers with the comic book(s).

JACK KIRBY
1963-1965
Referred to as the 'the King' and the man who got the X-MEN up and running.

WERNER ROTH
1965-1967 1968-1969
Also known as Jay Gavin. For part of his tenure, he worked over the layouts of Jack Kirby and Don Heck. His rendering of Marvel Girl leaves little doubt that he had a background in romance comics – including Millie the Model.

DON HECK
1967
With his Kirby-inspired graphics, he had a brief time on the title.

NEAL ADAMS
1969-1970
Adams' dynamic style and realistic renderings of the team won him many fans within the industry. The style was much imitated and future 'hot' artists cited his work as an influence.

DAVE COCKRUM
1975-1977 1981-1982
The first 'hot' artist on the title and co-creator of the new, second-generation X-MEN. For a long time, Cockrum was *the* artist of the X-MEN.

JOHN BYRNE
1977-1981
Without doubt, Byrne's concise, emotional and dynamic style was as responsible for the X-MEN's rise to success as Chris Claremont's writing. The talented team who co-plotted the title produced a book that was a quantum leap ahead of anything else being produced at the time.

PAUL SMITH
1983
Smith brought his animation skills to the UNCANNY X-MEN comic, with clear figurework and simple style. His artwork was well received by fans.

BIOGRAPHY
MAGNETO

1st Appearance: X-MEN #1

Of all the X-MEN's foes, Magneto is perhaps their greatest. Brought up in the horrors of the Auschwitz concentration camp, the man once known as Magnus saw the harshest brutalities of man and emerged from his time there as the only survivor of his family.

After the war, he made his way through the Iron Curtain countries where he met his wife Magda. He sired a daughter who later died. Magda became afraid of Magneto's emerging mutant powers and left him, not revealing that she was pregnant again. Her children would eventually become known as the heroes Quicksilver and the Scarlet Witch.

Magnus made his way to Israel where he first met Charles Xavier in the psychiatric hospital that was helping survivors of the Holocaust. Together they defeated Baron Strucker and Magnus claimed a hidden cache of Nazi gold for his own purposes.

Magnus vanished for many years and studied hard. He became aware of the rising persecution of mutants and remembered all too well the possible consequences of such hate. He swore that his kind would rise up to overthrow their persecutors, even if that meant *Homo superior* taking over the world from 'normal' *Homo sapiens*. Magneto's course of action put him at loggerheads with his old friend Charles Xavier, who had by now formed the X-MEN, and over the years they clashed on many occasions.

At one point Magneto created an artificial humanoid called Alpha with the aid of alien technology, but his creation turned on him and reverted the Master of Magnetism to infancy. The baby was entrusted to the care of Xavier's old friend Moira MacTaggert. Later, a Shi'ar agent returned Magneto to his old form.

After one battle with the X-MEN, in which the young X-Man Kitty Pryde was badly injured, Magneto began to question the moral ground on which he stood. He also found himself allied with the X-MEN and Earth's mightiest heroes in the event referred to as the first Secret Wars.

Magneto's growing interaction with humanity led to his softening his extreme ideas and he agreed to stand trial for his past crimes. The trial, in Paris, was invaded by the twins known as Fenris (Baron Strucker's children) and Xavier was badly injured. He asked Magneto to look after the NEW MUTANTS while he recuperated in outer space and reluctantly Magneto agreed.

Magnus was never comfortable with the role, but sought to continue the work that Xavier had started. The NEW MUTANTS distrusted him at first, but began to believe in him more than sometimes he did himself.

When the NEW MUTANTS were 'killed' (then resurrected) by the Beyonder, Magneto was powerless to help his charges and when later one of the New Mutants, Doug Ramsey, was killed in battle, Magneto realised that he had been too busy with other plans to carry out the job he had promised. He parted company with the team soon after.

Magneto became aware of a terrible truth. He found out that during his time as an infant, Moira MacTaggert had tried to alter his mind. As a result any decision he had made during the following years might not have bean as free as he had believed. Magneto was furious and attacked Moira, bringing him once again into conflict with his previous allies.

The government of the world issued the Magneto Protocols and with the X-MEN's help, his newly reformed Asteroid M was destroyed. It seemed that Magneto had died in the crash of the space-station but in fact he had survived. He was planning a safe haven for all mutants who wanted it and was willing to defend it to the death.

At the funeral of Illyana Rasputin, he appeared before the gathered X-Teams. In the ensuing battle Peter Rasputin (Colossus) decided to join Magneto. Shortly after, Charles and Magnus clashed once more. Xavier, as a last resort, wiped clean Magneto's mind. Peter declined to return to the team and took Magneto's body back to the sanctuary known as Avalon. Whether this is finally the end of the Master of Magnetism remains to be seen.

1st Appearance: UNCANNY X-MEN #221

BIOGRAPHY

Mr Sinister

Little is known about this mysterious figure, yet it has been revealed that he has monitored the X-MEN and particularly Scott Summers for decades. His exact interest has yet to be made clear, though many of his operations deal with the genetic potential of the Summers bloodline.

Mr Sinister secretly ran the orphanage where Scott Summers was confined after his parents' disappearance. He kept the young Scott Summers from achieving a successful adoption and continued to manipulate events even after Scott joined the X-MEN.

He created a clone of Jean Grey to be known as Madelyne Pryor (so named because of her 'prior' existence). Sinister was aware of Jean's own potential power, but as it seemed she had perished on the Moon (as Phoenix), Madelyne was to be his own pawn. At the moment of Jean/Phoenix's death, a portion of the Phoenix power was sent to restore the real Jean Grey's mind, but Jean's mind rejected the mental images of devastation that the Dark Phoenix had caused and the power sought out an alternative: her clone, Madelyne.

Madelyne Pryor was awakened from her 'sleep' and Sinister decided to use these unforeseen events to further manipulate Scott. Unaware of her real origins, Madelyne was sent to Alaska and began work with Scott's grandparents' airline. She believed herself to be the only survivor of a horrifying air-crash. Scott eventually visited his grandparents and was stunned to find someone who so closely resembled Jean.

Despite the interference of Mastermind, Scott and Madelyne were married and produced a son, Nathan Christopher. Thus was Sinister's dream fulfilled: the next generation of an all-powerful bloodline.

But the real Jean Grey was alive and when Scott returned to see her, Sinister attempted to kill Madelyne and kidnapped the young child. All records of their existence were destroyed.

Madelyne was finally rescued from Sinister's agents, the Marauder, and spent time with the X-MEN. Due to her hatred of Scott and his seeming betrayal of her by seeking out Jean, she eventually struck up a deal with demons from Limbo and obtained Nathan Christopher to sacrifice. In the ensuing battle Madelyne was killed and Nathan Christopher rescued.

Sinister's plan had been thwarted, but only for a time.

Since our first glimpses of the shadowy figure, he has extended his reach to include the whole Summers bloodline — past, present and future. This includes Alex Summers (Havok), the adult Nathan Christopher (Cable/Stryfe), Jean Grey and Rachel Summers (Jean and Scott's daughter from an alternate future).

Sinister has indicated he knows a lot about the future potential of the Summers' bloodline and its importance in the years to come. He has also hinted that it could involve the Legacy Virus and the possibility of a third Summers brother. However, anything that Mr Sinister says is laced with riddles and is questionable in its truth.

One thing is certain: Sinister's plans are far from over and the Summers clan is right in the middle of them.

JOHN ROMITA JNR
1983-1986
1993-onwards
Like his father, another Marvel artist, JR Jr proved his worth on the title on his original run and since his return to the UNCANNY title, his work is as popular as ever.

MARC SILVESTRI
1987-1989
Silvestri's work achieved a following as his style developed. His artwork remained popular and became more dynamic after he left the X-MEN to become the regular artist on WOLVERINE's solo series.

JIM LEE
1989-1992
In much the same way Byrne had a decade before, Lee brought a new clean and crisp style to the X-books and became the hottest artist in the business. He first worked on the UNCANNY title and then scored a major triumph on the record-smashin' multi-covered and poly-bagged X-MEN #1. Lee co-plotted the first three issues of the new X-MEN title with Claremont, and both plotted and drew the series for the rest of its initial year.

WHILCE PORTACIO
1991-1992
Portacio had been illustrating X-FACTOR, but was brought on board the X-Flagship whilst (Whilce?) Lee was busy. His complementary style gave the two main X-books a hugely successful start to the decade.

ANDY KUBERT
1992-onwards
Another second generation artist (taught by famous father Joe) who continued the '90s dramatic illustrations, building on the Lee/Portacio style but also bringing in his own. Building a strong fan following.

BIOGRAPHY
NEW MUTANTS
X-FORCE

Though the NEW MUTANTS group is now defunct, with some of its members in X-FORCE and others have spread across the world (and beyond). Hence it is worthy of inclusion in the X-MEN handbook.

Professor Xavier originally founded the school not as a base for a secret super-team, but as a home and school which would teach young mutants to fit into the world and learn to use their powers safely. When the X-MEN were lost in space and seemingly dead, the Professor brought together another generation of mutants. These, he decided, would not be new X-MEN, but would fulfil only his educational mission.

It later became apparent that this decision was influenced by a mysterious alien 'Brood' implanted in the Professor's body, slowly growing and taking over his body. With the Brood defeated, the Professor chose to keep the NEW MUTANTS together and continue their education. As ever, circumstances dictated that the new team would face off against several of the X-MEN's old foes.

When Xavier was critically injured he left Earth to recuperate and left the once-villainous Magneto to look after his charges. The NEW MUTANTS' reaction to this choice was mixed, with few believing that the Master of Magnetism had indeed changed his ways..

To his credit Magneto did his best, but he had other concerns and when one of the team, Doug Ramsey, was killed, he finally realised that he was not the man for the job.

The team finally disbanded, disillusioned with the price they were paying and questioning their own tactics. Several members of the team came together under the leadership of Cable to form the more aggressive and covert X-FORCE, which operates from an abandoned Indian reservation. Its membership has fluctuated wildly over the last few years.

PROMINENT NEW MUTANTS MEMBER BIOS

CANNONBALL
Sam Guthrie, with the ability to become a human 'rocket' and impervious to injury while blasting. Recently discovered to be an External (an immortal mutant). Currently leads X-FORCE.

KARMA
Xi'an Coy Manh, with the ability to possess people and control their actions through willpower. Now reluctantly working for her crooked uncle in Madripoor.

PSYCHE/MIRAGE
Danielle Moonstar, of Cheyenne descent, with the ability to project mental images such as someone's desire or worst nightmare. Honorary Valkyrie, now a possible member of the Mutant Liberation Front as Moonstar.

WOLFSBANE
Now a member of X-FACTOR, able to change into wolf form. Strict God-fearing background.

SUNSPOT
Roberto DaCosta, with the ability to super-charge his body with solar power. Left NEW MUTANTS shortly before the team disbanded. Later joined X-FORCE.

MAGIK
Illyana Rasputin. When Colossus' sister was lost in Limbo she aged seven years and acquired her mutant ability to teleport using light spheres. Also controlled arcane magic. Returned to infancy in defeating escaping demons from Limbo. She recently died of the Legacy Virus.

WARLOCK
Alien techno-shapechanger. Killed in action in Genosha.

MAGMA
Allison Crestmere, a.k.a. Amara Aquilla, appeared to come from a lost Roman outpost called Nova Roma. However, she was actually English and Nova Roma was in fact a creation of the Hellfire Club's Black Queen. Allison has the ability to control lava and rock.

CYPHER
Doug Ramsey, whose mutant ability was his superhuman linguistic skills. Killed in action saving Rahne's life.

TECH:

THE MANSION

Upper Levels

Professor Charles Xavier's School for Gifted Youngsters (or the Xavier Institute for Higher Learning as it has been renamed) is located at 1407 Graymalkin Lane just outside the town of Salem Center, New York.

The foundations of the original building date back to the 1700s when they were constructed near the Breakstone Lake by Charles Xavier's Dutch ancestors. Since then, the mansion and its grounds have always been in the Xavier family.

The visible parts of the building have been demolished and reconstructed on several occasions. On each subsequent repair, great efforts have been made to retain the historical and period feel of the exterior. This belies the extent of the

ICALS

Living Quarters

HISTORY

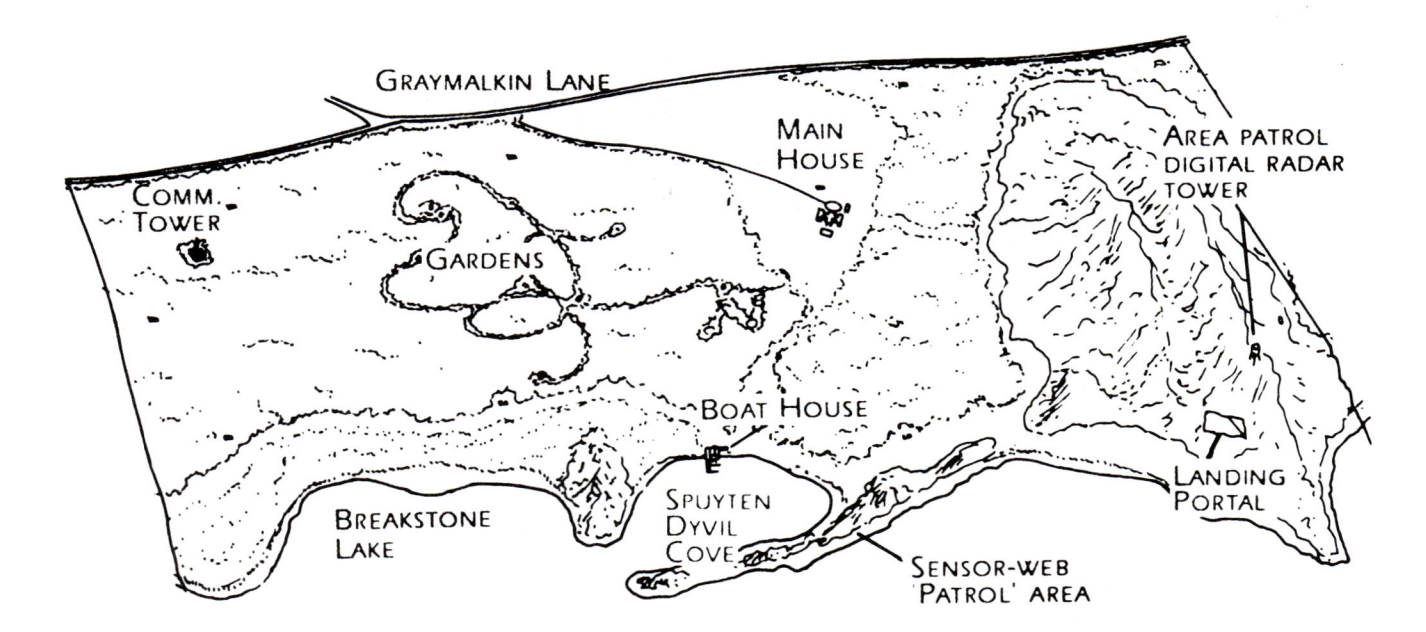

[Map showing: Graymalkin Lane, Comm. Tower, Gardens, Main House, Area Patrol Digital Radar Tower, Boat House, Breakstone Lake, Spuyten Dyvil Cove, Sensor-web 'Patrol' Area, Landing Portal]

technology that exists beyond and around these walls — a combination of the latest electronic developments and alien Shi'ar technology.

In the levels above ground, the X-MEN and guests have their own quarters, study facilities, recreation rooms and dining areas. Indeed, to a casual glance, the first impression would likely be that the mansion was a rather lavish and modern home or a wealthy private school.

Each X-Man's room is tailored to his or her needs and design wishes (within reason) so as to provide a genuine 'home' atmosphere away from the more treacherous hours spent on missions. These design wishes can vary greatly.

For the same reasons, the Mansion's Game Room is fully equipped with the latest technology from Earth and, in some cases, beyond. There is also a bar and quiet areas for those who wish simply to unwind.

LOWER LEVELS

All levels below ground are limited to the X-MEN and strictly authorised visitors. It is here under the mansion that the real heart of the X-MEN's base beats most strongly. From these lower levels, the teams' strategies and tactics can be worked out, defences can be devised and a higher degree of mutant training can be brought into play.

THE DANGER ROOM

The ultimate training area is the Mansion's Danger Room, a technological masterpiece and a unique battle-simulator. Using a mixture of holograms, solid light obstacles/threats and hi-tech electronics, any scenario can be programmed

The Essential Guide

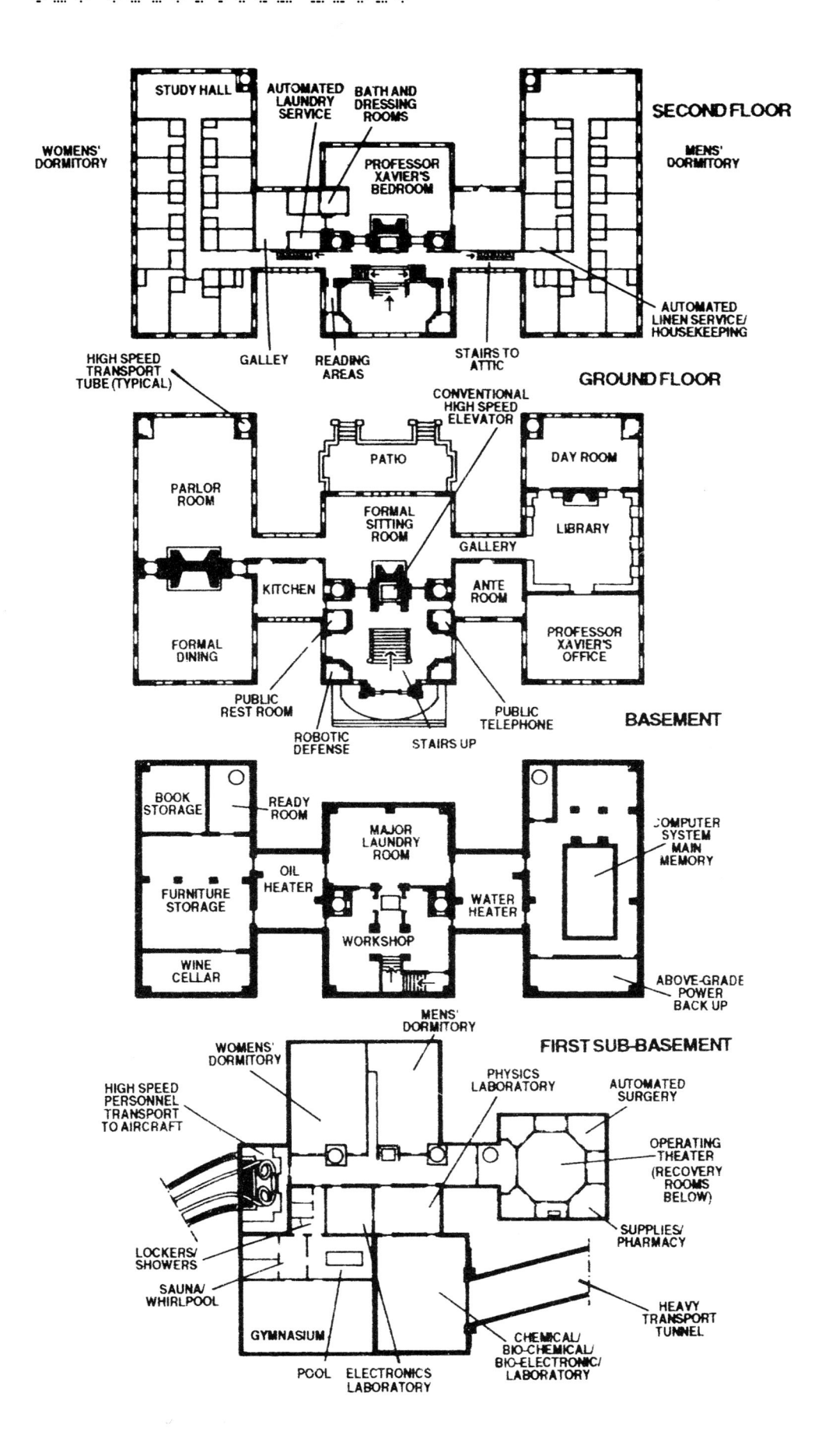

SECOND FLOOR

- STUDY HALL
- AUTOMATED LAUNDRY SERVICE
- BATH AND DRESSING ROOMS
- WOMENS' DORMITORY
- PROFESSOR XAVIER'S BEDROOM
- MENS' DORMITORY
- AUTOMATED LINEN SERVICE/ HOUSEKEEPING
- HIGH SPEED TRANSPORT TUBE (TYPICAL)
- GALLEY
- READING AREAS
- STAIRS TO ATTIC

GROUND FLOOR

- PARLOR ROOM
- CONVENTIONAL HIGH SPEED ELEVATOR
- PATIO
- DAY ROOM
- FORMAL SITTING ROOM
- LIBRARY
- GALLERY
- KITCHEN
- ANTE ROOM
- FORMAL DINING
- PROFESSOR XAVIER'S OFFICE
- PUBLIC REST ROOM
- PUBLIC TELEPHONE
- ROBOTIC DEFENSE
- STAIRS UP

BASEMENT

- BOOK STORAGE
- READY ROOM
- MAJOR LAUNDRY ROOM
- COMPUTER SYSTEM MAIN MEMORY
- FURNITURE STORAGE
- OIL HEATER
- WATER HEATER
- WINE CELLAR
- WORKSHOP
- ABOVE-GRADE POWER BACK UP

FIRST SUB-BASEMENT

- MENS' DORMITORY
- WOMENS' DORMITORY
- PHYSICS LABORATORY
- AUTOMATED SURGERY
- HIGH SPEED PERSONNEL TRANSPORT TO AIRCRAFT
- OPERATING THEATER (RECOVERY ROOMS BELOW)
- SUPPLIES/ PHARMACY
- LOCKERS/ SHOWERS
- SAUNA/ WHIRLPOOL
- HEAVY TRANSPORT TUNNEL
- GYMNASIUM
- CHEMICAL/ BIO-CHEMICAL/ BIO-ELECTRONIC/ LABORATORY
- POOL
- ELECTRONICS LABORATORY

6-7

TECHNICALS

into the room's computer memory and a game-play re-enacted.

There are 120 different levels, to cover the various degrees to which powers have been honed and hundreds of programs to stretch the agility, adaptability and quick thinking of individual or team players. Because some of the threats within the Danger Room are real, strict security is enforced during any given scenario. In the past members of the X-Teams have narrowly escaped serious injury by not taking the training sessions seriously.

The Danger Room is largely controlled by Shi'ar technology. An advanced 'Mobius strip' function allows players to feel as if they are travelling through a much bigger environment than the natural boundaries of the Danger Room itself. The actual room's operations are controlled from the neighbouring annex which overlooks the room and provides an ideal monitoring post for training exercises.

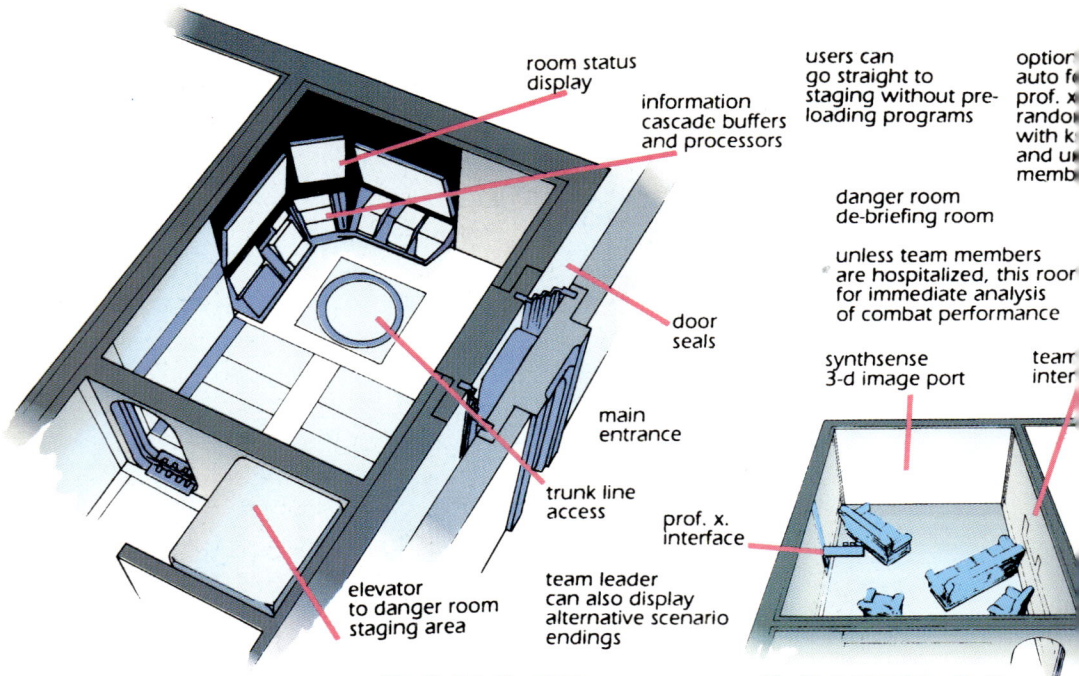

Labels (diagram):
- room status display
- information cascade buffers and processors
- door seals
- main entrance
- trunk line access
- elevator to danger room staging area
- users can go straight to staging without pre-loading programs
- option auto f prof. x rando with k and u memb
- danger room de-briefing room
- unless team members are hospitalized, this roor for immediate analysis of combat performance
- synthsense 3-d image port
- team inter
- prof. x. interface
- team leader can also display alternative scenario endings

DANGERroomCONTROLan

To the untrained eye it is a featureless room. To anyone who enters it, however, and engages its systems—it is clear that the Danger Room is the ultimate battle simulator.

Behind unassuming gray paneled walls exist a multitude of exercise and combat paraphernalia designed to put even the most well-trained mutant through their paces. (Laser cannons, omnium spring vices, pyrotechnic extension lances and sensory deprivation cocoons are only a handful of Shi'ar based hardware secreted within.) Recently combined with Shi'ar holographic technology, the Danger Room can assume a three dimensional interactive environment conducive to the constant refinement of teamwork vital to the X-Men's daily operations.

danger room control room area

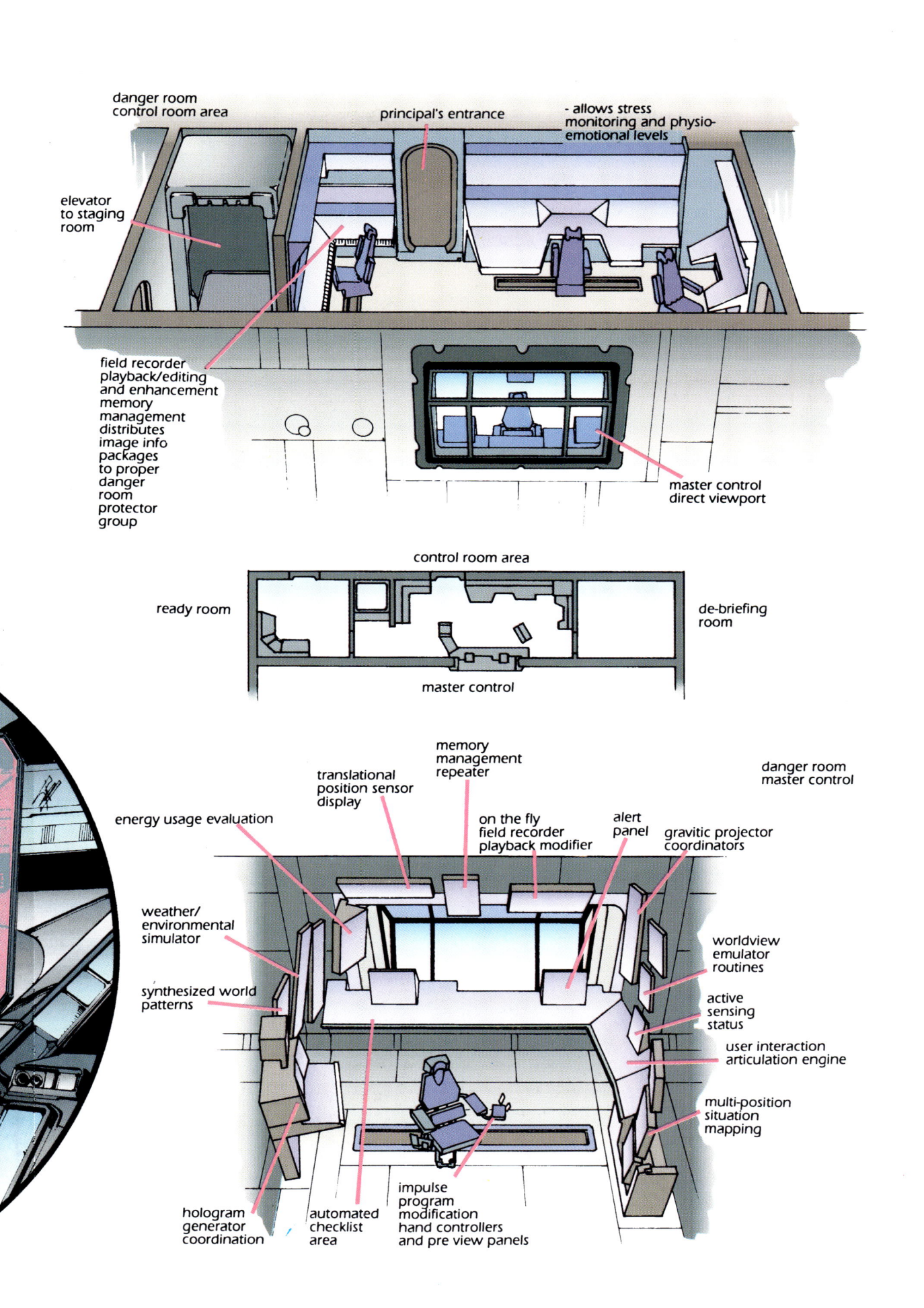

principal's entrance

- allows stress monitoring and physio-emotional levels

elevator to staging room

field recorder playback/editing and enhancement memory management distributes image info packages to proper danger room protector group

master control direct viewport

ready room — control room area — de-briefing room

master control

danger room master control

- translational position sensor display
- memory management repeater
- on the fly field recorder playback modifier
- alert panel
- gravitic projector coordinators
- energy usage evaluation
- weather/environmental simulator
- synthesized world patterns
- worldview emulator routines
- active sensing status
- user interaction articulation engine
- multi-position situation mapping
- hologram generator coordination
- automated checklist area
- impulse program modification hand controllers and pre view panels

BIOGRAPHY: ALLIES

There have been many allies of the X-MEN who have never been full-time members.

Presenting... some friends.

ALPHA FLIGHT
1st Appearance UNCANNY X-MEN #120
Canada's ex-official superteam first encountered the X-MEN when they tried to retrieve Wolverine back into their ranks. Alpha Flight members have subsequently cooperated with Wolverine and the X-MEN on various missions.

LILA CHENEY
1st Appearance NEW MUTANTS ANNUAL #1
Rock superstar in the Joan Jett, Pat Benatar or Allanah Myles mould, with the mutant ability to teleport on a galactic scale. Total babe!

VALERIE COOPER
1st Appearance UNCANNY X-MEN #176
Original government liaison for Freedom Force and later X-FACTOR.

DEPARTMENT H
1st mentioned in UNCANNY X-MEN #139
Top-Secret Canadian government agency and creators of ALPHA FLIGHT. Recently shown to be involved with the creation of Wolverine's adamantium skeleton and enhancements on mercenaries Maverick and Sabretooth.

ALEYTIS (LEE) FORRESTER
1st Appearance UNCANNY X-MEN #143
Friend of Scott Summers and ex-love interest of Magneto. Current whereabouts unknown.

GATEWAY
1st Appearance UNCANNY X-MEN #227
Mystical Aborigine whose power creates teleport gates with his bullroarer. Assisted X-MEN when they relocated to Australia.

STEVIE HUNTER
1st Appearance UNCANNY X-MEN #139
Kitty Pryde's dance teacher and assistant trainer to the NEW MUTANTS. Close friend of the X-MEN with high security clearance to their mansion.

IMPERIAL GUARD
1st Appearance X-MEN (first series) #107
Guards of the Sh'iar monarchy. Clashed with the X-MEN on several occasions (most notably in the Phoenix tragedy), but have more often aided the mutants in crises of galactic importance.

KA-ZAR
1st Appearance X-MEN (first series) #10
Born Lord Kevin Plunder. Now lives in the Savage Land, a forgotten jungle under the Antarctic with wife Shanna and sabre-toothed Zabu.

LILANDRA NERAMANI
1st Appearance X-MEN (first series) #97
Leader of the Sh'iar Empire in a distant galaxy and love interest of Charles Xavier, recently faced upheaval in her stellar Empire. Recently conquered the Kree galactic Empire.

LOCKHEED
1st Appearance UNCANNY X-MEN #166
Totally cool, small purple dragon that accompanied Kitty Pryde home from the X-MEN's encounter with the Brood in outer space. Currently with Kitty in EXCALIBUR.

DR. MOIRA MacTAGGERT
1st Appearance X-MEN (first series) #96
First believed by the X-MEN to be Professor Xavier's housekeeper, but later to be revealed as his ex-fiancee and trusted friend as well as a genetics expert herself. She was held responsible by Magneto for altering his mind and therefore influencing later decisions Magneto made. Currently working on a cure for the Legacy Virus on Muir Island. Romantically involved with Banshee.

MORLOCKS
1st Appearance UNCANNY X-MEN #169
Misunderstood mutants who lived in the sewers of New York. Clashed with the X-MEN several times but with Storm as leader, alliances were formed. Most Morlocks were slaughtered in the Mutant Massacre.

ROMA
1st Appearance CAPTAIN BRITAIN #1
Responsible for the creation of Captain Britain with her father Merlin. She is guardian of the multiverse and restored

ANTAGONISTS

the X-MEN to life after they saved her from the clutches of the Adversary. Also helped in the creation of EXCALIBUR.

STARJAMMERS
1st Appearance X-MEN (first series) #107
A group of swashbuckling inter-galactic adventurers led by Corsair (Major Christopher Summers, Scott and Alex's long-lost father). Other prominent members include the aliens Ch'od, Hepzibah and Raza and the earth-born superhuman Binary (Coral Danvers).

MARIKO YASHIDA
1st Appearance UNCANNY X-MEN #118
Head of the Yashida clan and at one time Wolverine's bride-to-be. Mastermind's manipulations and the tainted honour of her clan's name came between them. Recently killed by Matsuo Tsurayaba of the Ninja assassins, The Hand.

And of course there have been many who would stand against our merry mutants.

Presenting.....some of the fiends!

ACOLYTES
1st Appearance X-MEN (2nd series) #1 1991
Self-proclaimed disciples of Magneto. The Master of Magnetism gave them sanctuary on Asteroid M. Acolyte leader Fabian Cortez betrayed Magneto and tried to make the remaining Acolytes serve him after Magneto's apparent death, but they rebelled against him.

APOCALYPSE
1st Appearance X-FACTOR #5
The mysterious 'mutant master of evolution' whose impact on the lives of the X-Teams seems to indicate he has not only been around for centuries but will be for centuries to come. Creator of Archangel's wings and responsible for the infection of Nathan Christopher Summers which led to the infant eventually becoming Cable.

BROOD
1st Appearance UNCANNY X-MEN #155
Space-monsters with the nasty habit of implanting eggs inside their victims who then act as living/dying hosts.

TREVOR FITZROY
1st Appearance UNCANNY X-MEN #281
Fugitive from Bishop's future time-line and current member of the Upstarts.

HELLFIRE CLUB
1st Appearance UNCANNY X-MEN #129
Genuine high society club which hid the sinister agenda of its Inner Circle. Many of that original circle are now dead or out of action and have bbeen replaced by a 'next generation' of rich and morally dubious members, led by the mutant Shinobi Shaw.

MASTERMIND
1st Appearance X-MEN (first series) #4
Jason Wyngarde, founding member of the Brotherhood of Evil Mutants and ally of the Hellfire Club's Inner Circle, Mastermind was responsible for the events which led to the creation of Dark Phoenix. Phoenix nearly destroyed his mind. He recently died after making his peace with Jean Grey. He was another victim of the Legacy Virus.

MOJO
1st Appearance LONGSHOT LIMITED SERIES #3
Gross, obnoxious, power-obsessed, ratings-seeking, spineless, kidnapping, megalomaniac... and those were just his good points! Recently killed in a rebellion by his successor Mojo II.

MYSTIQUE
1st Appearance as Mystique: Ms MARVEL #18
Past and present opponent of the X-MEN who has aided them on occasion. Ex-leader of FREEDOM FORCE, recently revealed as Nightcrawler's mother. Unofficial foster mother of Rogue and mother of the X-MEN's enemy Graydon Creed.

STRYFE
1st Appearance as adult UNCANNY X-MEN #294
Clone of Nathan Christopher Summers. Archenemy of Cable and leader of the original Mutant Liberation Front. Nearly killed Professor X in an assassination attempt. See entry on Cable.

UPSTARTS
1st Appearance UNCANNY X-MEN #281
Led by a mysterious 'Gamesmaster' this mutant version of the infamous Billionaire Boys Club seek the ultimate prize with points being allocated for the number of kills each member achieves. Members include Shinobi Shaw of the Hellfire Club, Trevor Fitzroy from Bishop's alternative future, Graydon Creed of the mutant-hating Friends of Humanity, and the powerful mutant Siena Blaze. Can't they just play Scrabble and be done with it?

THE BLACKBIRDS & HANGAR

THE HANGAR

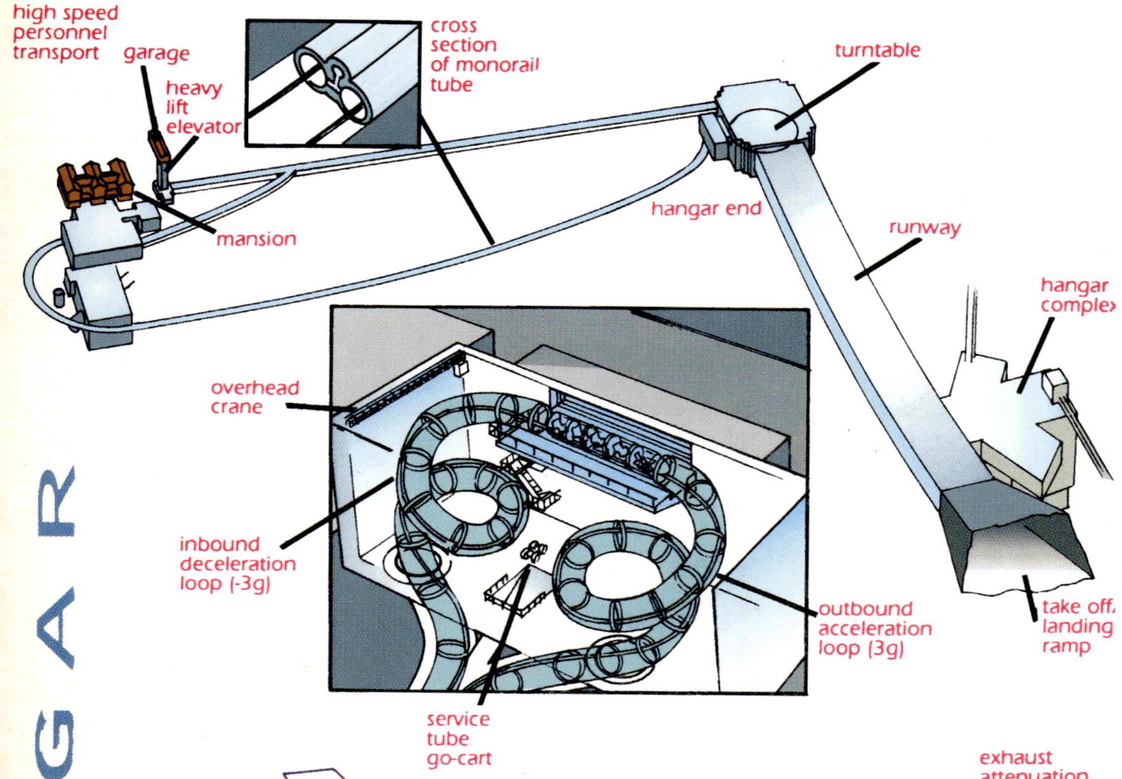
high speed
personnel
transport
garage
heavy
lift
elevator
cross
section
of monorail
tube
turntable
mansion
hangar end
runway
hangar
complex
overhead
crane
inbound
deceleration
loop (-3g)
outbound
acceleration
loop (3g)
take off/
landing
ramp
service
tube
go-cart

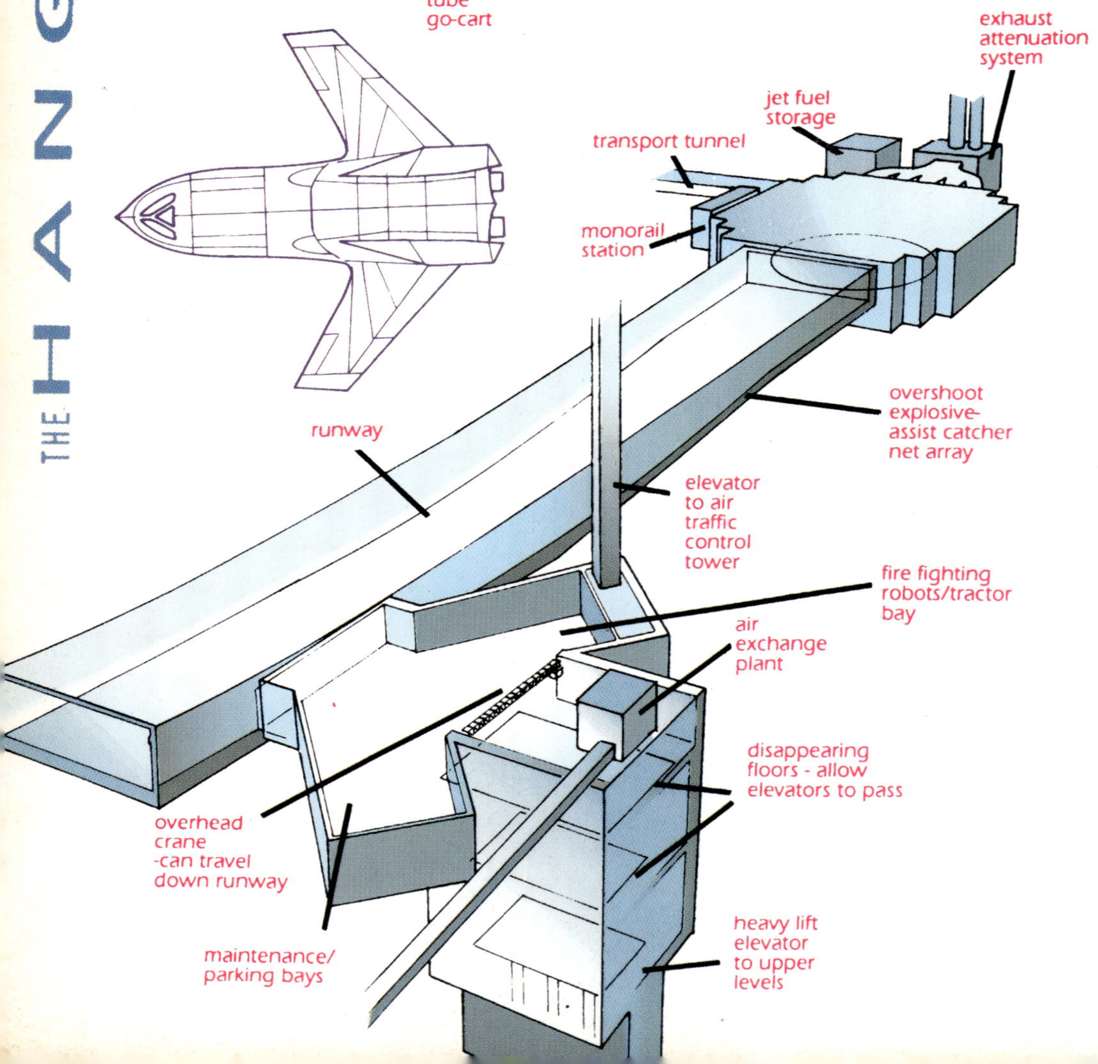
exhaust
attenuation
system
jet fuel
storage
transport tunnel
monorail
station
overshoot
explosive-
assist catcher
net array
runway
elevator
to air
traffic
control
tower
fire fighting
robots/tractor
bay
air
exchange
plant
disappearing
floors - allow
elevators to pass
overhead
crane
-can travel
down runway
heavy lift
elevator
to upper
levels
maintenance/
parking bays

One of the other major features of the Mansion and its sub-levels is the housing area of the X-MEN's two Blackbird aircraft. Blackbird Blue is based on the original aircraft used by the team and its design, at least externally, is fairly close to that of a conventional Blackbird military plane, although the technology it uses is, of course, much more sophisticated.

Blackbird Gold is the latest of Forge's designs to be used, although the two aircraft are comparable in speed and technology.

The craft can be used for short- or long-haul missions in a variety of climates, travelling at trans-sonic speeds, and are capable of carrying the members of the current team plus guests if necessary.

A high speed monorail runs from the mansion to the hangars and the Blackbirds exit the area from the far side of the Mansion grounds. The aircrafts' stealth abilities cut takeoff and touch-down noise to a minimum. Though a runway exists for the two planes, both have the ability for Vertical Take-Off and Landing (V.T.O.L.).

1st Appearance: X-MEN #1

BIOGRAPHY

PROFESSOR X

Charles Xavier is one of the most powerful telepaths on Earth. His powers manifested themselves at a young age. He accidentally read the mind of his half-brother Cain Marko, who had just been beaten by Karl Marko, Xavier's step-father. Cain realised what had happened and thought that Charles had acted deliberately.

As Charles grew up, one side-effect of his growing powers was loss of his hair. He studied in New York and London, specialising in genetics and biology. At Oxford he met Moira MacTaggert, also a scholar in genetics. After Moira's divorce came through, the couple planned to marry, but Charles was drafted and sent to Asia. He served with his step-brother Cain. Together they found a secret cave and the lost temple of Cyttorak. Cain stole a glowing gem which was transformed into a super-powered being (later known as the Juggernaut). A sudden enemy bombardment caused a cave-in. Both Cain and Xavier survived.

Moira, without explanation, called off their engagement and heartbroken Charles began to travel the world. While visiting Tibet, he encountered a town controlled by an alien called Lucifer. Using his telepathic abilities, Xavier freed the town, but the alien retaliated by crushing Xavier's legs under a huge stone block.

Virtually a recluse in his New York State mansion, Charles eventually crossed professional paths again with Moira MacTaggert and they discussed the idea of setting up a school for young mutants with special powers.

Professor John Grey approached Charles when his daughter Jean seemed greatly disturbed.

Xavier realised that she was a mutant whose own telepathic powers had emerged following the death of her friend. He eased her pain and erected psychic shields to protect her mind. Years afterwards the FBI began to open investigations into super-powered mutants, spurred on by an incident involving the young Scott Summers. Xavier approached an FBI agent, Fred Duncan, and proposed that he could train these new mutants. Soon, Xavier was bringing together his first team of X-MEN.

Over the years Xavier saw the X-MEN grow, learn, live and die. The faces of his students may have changed but his goal has always been to teach those in need of help and work towards a future where humans and mutants can live together without hate.

More recently, some of the X-MEN have called into question some of the dubious methods Xavier has employed as a means to that end. In Xavier's battle with Magneto, shortly after Illyana Rasputin's death, Xavier robbed Magneto of his mind. Even Charles Xavier is finding his dream on the edge of becoming a nightmare...

TECHNICALS

The Danger Room can project a wild and wide assortment of threats.

THE WAR ROOM

With the world becoming more and more violent, particularly for mutants, it has become ever more necessary carefully to monitor events on both local and international scales.

The X-MEN's War Room is capable of doing that to an extremely high degree, constantly monitoring signals which can range in origin from sources as diverse as CNN and the CIA through to the BBC and S.H.I.E.L.D. The team can instantly find information, live, from any place with broadcast technology.

Such information can be invaluable when travelling to a far-off country or unknown area. Such information can be compiled and stored and used for briefing on missions. Thousands of files on current operatives, allies and enemies can be instantly retrieved for the same purposes.

THE ESSENTIAL GUIDE

As well as this 'hacking' ability, the War Room also allows less covert, but equally secure, communication with allies such as the Avengers, Reed Richards or, when necessary, the government.

The latest technology, combined with Shi'ar and Forge's own designs, make tracing of any security leak back to the Mansion impossible for outside intelligence.

CEREBRO

Originally designed for boosting telepathic ability for the process of locating and tracing emerging mutants (who might need help and training), Cerebro was the ultimate 'mutant detector'.

Whether due to environmental changes or simply the dramatic increase in the mutant population, Cerebro has often been pushed to its limitations. However, the computer is still used when extra range and power are needed in tracking a given target.

Cerebro was built for use by trained telepaths, though it is possible for the system to be used by non-psis with

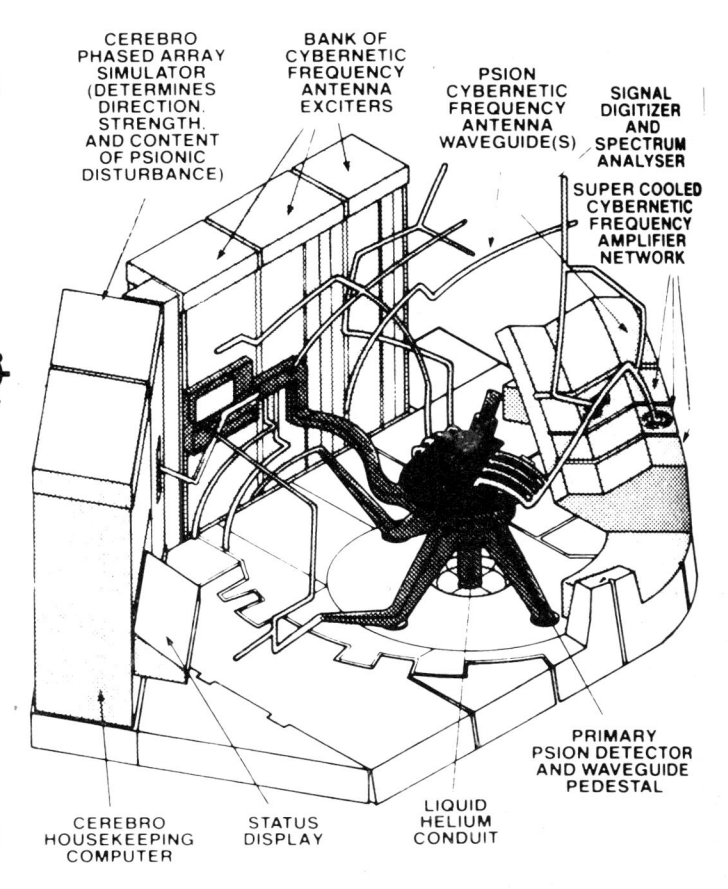

Labels on diagram: CEREBRO PHASED ARRAY SIMULATOR (DETERMINES DIRECTION, STRENGTH, AND CONTENT OF PSIONIC DISTURBANCE); BANK OF CYBERNETIC FREQUENCY ANTENNA EXCITERS; PSION CYBERNETIC FREQUENCY ANTENNA WAVEGUIDE(S); SIGNAL DIGITIZER AND SPECTRUM ANALYSER; SUPER COOLED CYBERNETIC FREQUENCY AMPLIFIER NETWORK; PRIMARY PSION DETECTOR AND WAVEGUIDE PEDESTAL; LIQUID HELIUM CONDUIT; STATUS DISPLAY; CEREBRO HOUSEKEEPING COMPUTER.

Cerebro should only be used by skilled psis.

BIOGRAPHY

1st US Appearance: NEW MUTANTS ANNUAL #2

PSYLOCKE

Betsy Braddock is the twin sister of Brian Braddock, Captain Britain. She first encountered the X-MEN when she was captured by the inter-dimensional television magus known as Mojo. She chose to remain with the X-MEN on her return to Earth, now equipped with bionic eyes. When Sabretooth came calling during the Mutant Massacre of the Morlocks, she proved her worth and became a fully fledged X-Man.

She fought and died alongside the team when they faced the evil Adversary in Dallas. When Roma, the guardian of the multiverse resurrected the team, Psylocke relocated with them to Australia.

When several of the X-MEN, under Psylocke's influence, decided to enter the Siege Perilous, a portal through which they could be cleansed and begin new lives, the Betsy Braddock that everyone knew and loved ceased to exist.

What happened during the months she was missing remains a mystery. It seems that she psychically merged with an Oriental assassin called Kwannon, taking on more Oriental physical features and learning impressive Ninja techniques.

Recently another woman claiming to be Betsy turned up at the Mansion. Psi-probes indicate that the personalities of the two Betsys are virtually inseparable, each containing half of the other and impossible to distinguish. The second Betsy, codenamed Revanche, was recently found to be infected with the Legacy Virus and decided to 'go out fighting' rather than stay hospitalised for research.

sufficient training. Over the years, the system has been damaged and rebuilt and now functions to a higher degree than ever before. Fortunately, or unfortunately, the need to seek out unknown mutants is less common, as in recent years — potential enemies and allies have sought out the X-MEN themselves!

Cerebro: the computer in action.

PROFESSOR XAVIER'S READY ROOM

Until recently the very existence of this room was a secret held by Xavier himself. He used the Ready Room as his own 'sanctum sanctorum', a place where he could be alone. But the Ready Room is much more than a glorified study. If the Mansion has a nerve centre, then this room is surely the place.

From this location, Professor Xavier can control every system in the Mansion and access files that are for his eyes only. Communication in and out of this room is secured to a higher degree than anywhere else in the complex.

So sensitive is the room and the potential information/control it contains that any unauthorised entry would meet with an instant expulsion. Any attack

Technicals

threatening to compromise the Ready Room's security would automatically engage the self-destruct programs.

In recent months, Xavier has allowed limited access to the senior members of the X-Teams as a way of keeping them (and himself) in touch with the 'big picture'.

The Medi-Lab

Once little more than a surgery/operating area (albeit specialised for mutants), the Medi-Lab is now one of the most advanced medical facilities on Earth.

With the aid of Shi'ar technology and cutting edge programs, the lab can provide full-scale treatment for individual injuries of physical or psi nature. Should the need arise, as it has unfortunately done in the past, large numbers of casualties can also be treated when necessary.

Morlock Tunnels

Underneath the streets of New York there is a network of largely unexplored tunnels which were occupied by the mutant outcasts known as the Morlocks. Despite the fact that virtually all these inhabitants have either vanished or been killed, the tunnels remain largely intact and there is a tunnel connection point underneath the Mansion itself.

This entrance is kept securely locked and monitored, as it is a potential weak

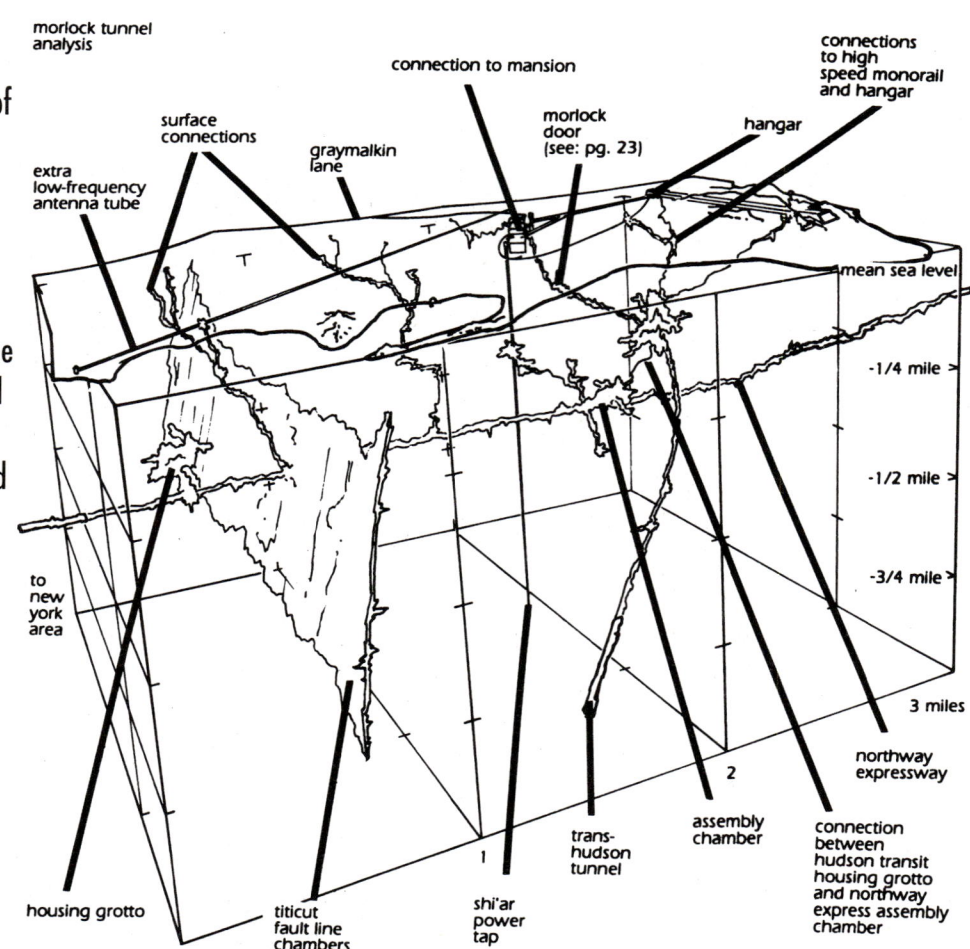

BIOGRAPHY
ROGUE

1st Appearance: AVENGERS ANNUAL #10

Little is known of Rogue's childhood, though it is clear from her accent that she comes from the southern banks of the Mississippi River, somewhere in Caldecott County. So far she has not revealed her real name to any of her current team-mates.

Rogue first experienced her mutant power when she shared her first kiss with a boy named Cody Robbins. Suddenly she discovered her mind was full of Robbins' memories. Unable to cope with the experience, she fled. After a time, the boy's memories faded and Rogue began to realise that her mutant powers caused her to absorb the personality and memories of whoever came into contact with her. Her powers were also uncontrollable. Rogue joined the second incarnation of the Brotherhood of Evil Mutants and their leader Mystique came to see Rogue as a surrogate daughter.

On a mission to steal the superhuman abilities of the original Ms Marvel (Carol Danvers), something went wrong with the absorbing process and Rogue found that the transfer was permanent. Rogue now possessed the powers of Ms Marvel. From that point on, Rogue grew more and more mentally unstable, never completely sure whether her reactions and choices were being influenced by aspects of Carol Danvers' personality. The Brotherhood could not help her so finally she sought the help of Professor Xavier, mentor of the team that she had frequently faced in battle.

At first, the X-MEN were appalled that an enemy was being treated under their roof, doubly so because Carol Danvers was friend of the team. In time, though, Rogue proved herself as a valuable and trustworthy member of the team. When Mystique asked Rogue to return with her, Rogue declined and made a decision to stay with the X-MEN. While she is now better adjusted to her powers, she is still unable to control her absorbing abilities.

When the mutant Gambit joined the X-MEN, she began to fall for the smooth-talking Cajun adventurer, but her condition means working more slowly and carefully at a romantic relationship.

Rogue is currently a member of the X-MEN's Blue Team.

BIOGRAPHY

SABRETOOTH

1st Appearance: IRON FIST #4

Perhaps even more feral than Wolverine, Sabretooth has joined the X-MEN in an effort to control his more bestial instincts. In fact, Sabretooth is confined at the X-MEN mansion lest he turn against them.

Little is known of the ex-assassin and mercenary. It seems likely that he was a member of a covert team that included Wolverine and the soldier Maverick. Both Wolverine and Sabretooth suffer from implants that distorted their memories and indicates that they were parts of the same secret experimental project. Wolverine believed for a long time that Sabretooth had killed his beloved Indian fiancée. Later he discovered that this was yet another result of the implants. However, the hate between Sabretooth and Wolverine is very real and has frequently exploded in savage fights. Sabretooth has also battled the X-MEN repeatedly, and once belonged to Mr Sinister's Marauders.

Xavier's mind-probing of the X-MEN's guest indicated that the man, Victor Creed, was horribly abused as a child, his father being both disgusted and frightened by his son's animal-like mutation.

Further revelations indicate that Creed was also married to the mutant Mystique, though he was not aware of her true identity. Sabretooth, just prior to taking up residence at the X-MEN's mansion, was hired to kill Mystique by Graydon Creed, a man claiming to be Sabretooth and Mystique's son. Graydon Creed was defeated but managed to kill Sabretooth's companion Birdy, who might have been the only person who could help release Sabretooth's inner torment. It was for this reason that Sabretooth sought the help of Charles Xavier.

Xavier decreed that Sabretooth should be treated for his mental condition at the mansion, much to the alarm of the X-MEN. However, Xavier pointed out that Wolverine (who had recently departed the team) had experienced the same sort of problems when he first became an X-Man and had gone on to become the firmest of friends and allies. Reluctantly, to say the least, the X-MEN accepted Xavier's decision, but quite rightly (by Sabretooth's own admission) they have no real reason to trust him.

In truth, Sabretooth could prove more dangerous as a team-mate than as the enemy he has been for many years.

CLAW TO CLAW WITH SABERTOOTH!

**1st Appearance:
GIANT SIZE X-MEN #1**

BIOGRAPHY
STORM

Ororo Munroe can trace her ancestry back through countless ages and a line of African witch-priestesses. She was born, though, in the heart of New York City. When she was six months old, she and her parents moved to Cairo, Egypt. Five years later their house was destroyed by a bomb. Her parents were killed and Ororo was trapped in the rubble and to this day she suffers claustrophobia.

For the next six years, Ororo became a sneak thief working for a man named Achmed el-Gibar and eventually became his star pupil. At the age of twelve, she felt herself drawn south and eventually found her way to the Serengeti plains, the home of her ancestors. Her mutant abilities began to manifest themselves and she realised that she was able to control the weather. For years she used this ability to help the people of the plains, but a visit by Professor Xavier (looking for a second generation of X-MEN) prompted her to use her abilities to make a difference on a wider scale.

During a mission with her team-mate Rogue, Storm was hit by a blast from an experimental gun designed by the mutant inventor Forge, but fired by government agent Henry Gyrich. Storm barely survived and found herself stripped of her powers. She refused Forge's offers of help.

For a while, Storm left the team and returned to her homeland in an effort to come to terms with her current state. She returned to lead the X-MEN and proved herself a master of strategy and cunning, the talents learned on the streets of Cairo coming in very useful.

When the Adversary, an evil mystical being, took control of Forge's home, the glass skyscraper called Eagle Plaza, the X-MEN and Freedom Force (the Brotherhood of Evil Mutants as a bonafide government team) found themselves outmatched. For deliberate reasons, the Adversary removed Storm and Forge from the game, delivering them to a pure new world in another dimension. They spent a year there, discovering the land and searching for a way back. Finally they devised a plan to revive Storm's powers and send them home, where mere seconds had passed.

The world believed the X-MEN to have perished. In fact, they had moved their base of operations to Australia. Some time later Storm was kidnapped by an egg-shaped armoured villain called Nanny who reverted Storm's form to that of a child. It was during this time that Storm first encountered Gambit.

Later, back in her true form, she returned to the X-MEN and faced the wrath of such villains as The Shadow King and Magneto.

She currently leads the X-MEN's Gold Team.

An emergency exit to the tunnels.

link to the Mansion, should the area be compromised. The link has not been severed because, ironically, it could also be an excellent emergency escape route should the need arise.

SECURITY

The Mansion and its grounds are in a secluded location approximately five miles from Salem Center, the closest town. It is a lake front property; therefore, there are significant natural defences against some forms of attack.

Long range scanners should detect any approaching vehicle or person on either the roads or the land outside the complex. Anti-acceleration pads prevent any vehicles being able to ram the main gates and all entrances and exits from the grounds are monitored both visually and in audio.

As with many other aspects of the inner and lower Mansion, the security has been enhanced by Shi'ar technology. This include sensitive force-fields, motion detectors, virtual reality scanners and a tight sensory web. All invited guests are issued passes which allow them access to certain areas. However, many parts of the Mansion can only be entered when in the company of someone with high-security clearance, such as members of the X-MEN teams or selected allies.

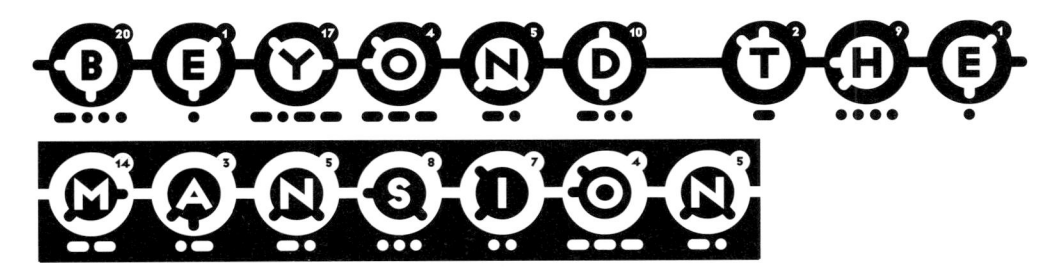

BEYOND THE MANSION

Through the Mansion is the X-MEN's main base, they also have several other annexes that they are able to use.

One of these is Muir Island, off the Scottish coast, which houses the medical research facilities of Dr Moira MacTaggert. The island was virtually levelled during the X-Teams' confrontation with the being known as the Shadow King, but much was salvaged from the destruction and now the island's research station is better than ever. As well as being at the forefront of biological and genetic research, Moira's laboratories are fully equipped for medical emergencies.

Muir Island is currently devoting much of its work to the search for a cure for the Legacy Virus — a virus introduced by Stryfe, the terrorist from the future, that is lethal to mutants. Moira, Forge (in Washington DC) and Henry McCoy (Beast) are considered to be at the forefront of research into the disease. Although Muir Island is part of the X-MEN's extended base of operations, the actual connection between the publicly-recognised research department and the mutant teams' interests is not known to the public.

. The island is also currently used by EXCALIBUR as their main base. Sean Cassidy, who was the X-MAN codenamed Banshee and is now Moira's lover, spends a lot of time there, for obvious reasons.

The Massachusetts Academy, the private school that was the former base of the villainous White Queen, is set to re-open as the base of a new team currently referred to as GENERATION X and will operate as a school for young mutants. Training at the Mansion would now be inappropriate with the number of X-MEN currently in residence and the potential dangers they could attract. Professor Xavier has approached Sean Cassidy to head the school.

THE ANIMATED X-MEN

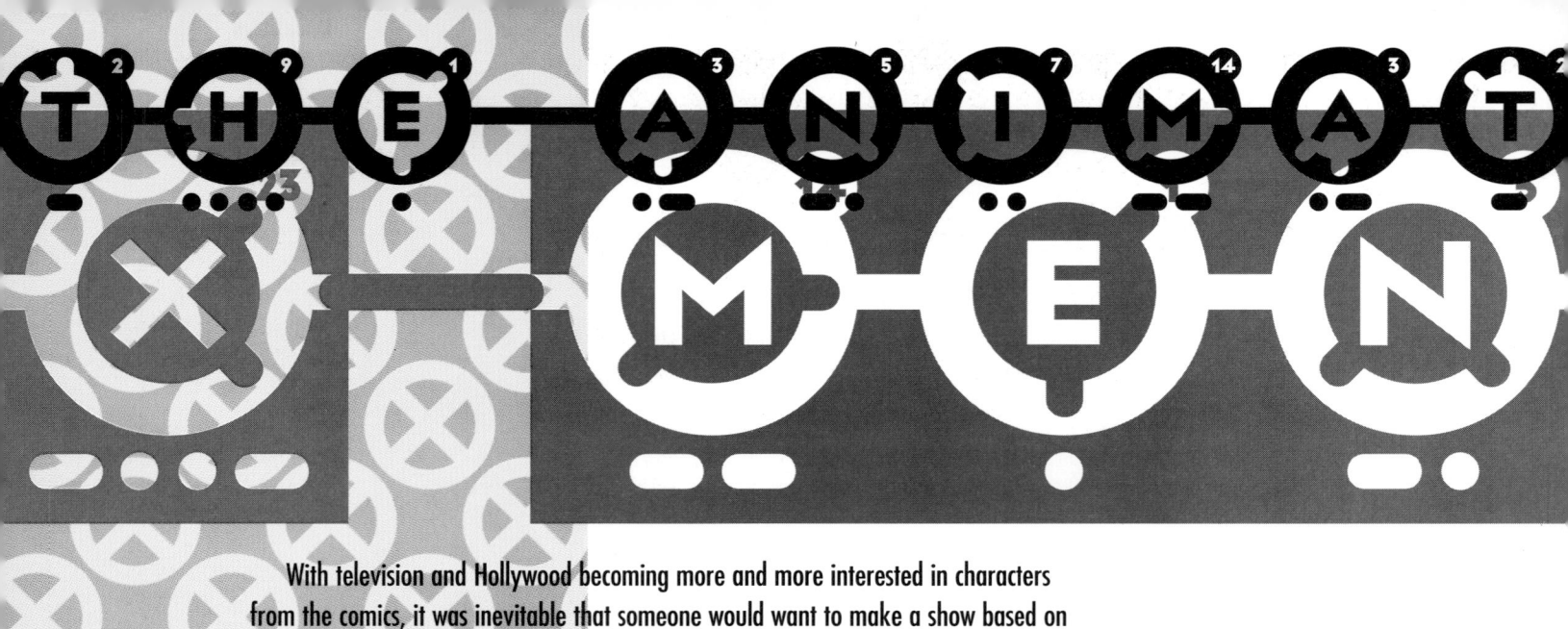

With television and Hollywood becoming more and more interested in characters from the comics, it was inevitable that someone would want to make a show based on the exploits of the most successful comic in the business. The questions were simply: who, when and would it be any good?

Over the past few years some attempts were made, but none proved to have quite the magic needed. The X-MEN did guest-star in the 'Spiderman And His Amazing Friends' animated show (which introduced us to another character, Firestar, who would later appear in the Marvel comic book universe) but that was primarily because Spidey's other amazing friend was Iceman.

There were many production companies interested in the project. The rights were won by Saban Entertainment who signed the deal with Marvel in 1992, almost a full year before it first hit American screens.

When the series was first shown on America's Fox Network, it rapidly became one of the most popular animated shows

ED SERIES

X-MEN

ever and set all kinds of records. The show, screened on Saturday mornings, created a major buzz within the industry and renewed interest in the Marvel comic book. After thirty years on the printed page, the X-MEN had conquered television.

Currently 65 episodes are in production, of which the first two seasons, 26 episodes, are confirmed for British television. The success of the animated show has

The X-MEN as featured in the cartoon series from Saban Entertainment.

also brought the planned live-action X-MEN movie project much closer to reality. As with all comic-to-TV adaptations, certain changes are made and although — somewhat remarkably — they are few in this case, they bear explaining.

Marvel have been chronicling the X-MEN's adventures for over thirty years. That's a long time for readers to become familiar with any characters. For a prime-time animated series, setting the scene for potential new fans is important. For that reason, subtle changes have to be made to simplify long-winded explanations. Besides, these explanations could make great stories later on, when viewers take various character traits as given.

For the series, a prime case is Jubilee. In the first five minutes, we know all the important facts about this young mutant (at least for the moment!). To recount the history of the character as it appeared in the standard Marvel Universe would take a series on its own (or see her bio!).

So accept that if you watch the series first, then read the comic, certain things will be different and vice versa.

It's what the cosmic entity known as the Watcher would explain as a 'What If World': a world in which events have subtly different outcomes, thus making the characters slightly different. It shouldn't spoil the enjoyment; it should add to it.

In the next pages we present a list of the episodes (in order) for the first two series of the animated series.

The First Transmission Date (FTD) indicates the first time the individual episode was screened to American audiences. Each episode was/is repeated several times on different dates.

SEASON 1

1. NIGHT OF THE SENTINELS – PART ONE
Written by Mark Edward Edens
FTD: 31st October 1992

A young girl sits at the top of her stairs and listens to her adoptive parents discussing the pros and cons of having registered their 'daughter' under the Mutant Registration Act. Jubilation Lee doesn't wait to hear the outcome and narrowly avoids capture by a Sentinel robot sent to detain her.

The giant robot follows her trail to the local shopping mall where several members of the X-MEN, in plainclothes, are spending some free time. The robot captures Jubilee but Storm, Rogue and Gambit detain the Sentinel long enough for Cyclops to destroy it.

Jubilee awakes in the X-MEN's mansion and after an impromptu prowl, is introduced to the team which also includes Wolverine, Jean Grey, Beast, Morph and their leader Professor X.

Information taken from the Sentinel's head indicates that it was working from details known only to those involved with the Mutant Registration Act. Professor X decides that the relevant files should be destroyed. But what's wrong with Morph?

Note: In the original script, the character of Morph was simply called Changeling.

2. NIGHT OF THE SENTINELS – PART TWO
Written by Mark Edward Edens
FTD: 7th November 1992

Jubilee is held prisoner by Gyrich, who tries to convince her to give him information on the X-MEN.

The raid on the Federal building has gone well and Morph's premonition seems to have been unfulfilled. The files are destroyed but on the way out, the team is attacked by Sentinels. Morph takes the full impact of a Sentinel blast and the Beast is also injured.

Cyclops (Scott) has to make a command decision as the odds tilt against them. He orders the team to withdraw, leaving Morph apparently dead and the Beast captured. Wolverine is furious with Cyclops and refuse to deal with him after the withdrawal.

Gyrich is informed by the White House and the President herself that the Mutant Registration Act is to be abolished and the Sentinel program may be next. Gyrich refuses to let the project cease and sees a way to ensure it continues...

3. ENTER MAGNETO
Written by Jim Carlson & Terrence McDonnell
FTD: 27th November 1992

The Beast sits alone in his cell reading, ignoring the taunts of the redneck guards. There are noises from outside, which the Beast presumes to be made by the X-MEN. In fact, his would-be rescuer is the Master of Magnetism, Magneto, who asks the Beast to follow him.

However, the Beast wants to stay in prison until trial, in an effort to draw attention to the X-MEN's honourable aims. Magneto scoffs, telling him mankind cannot live with itself, never mind mutants. At the trial Wolverine spots an old enemy, Sabretooth.

Xavier has met Magneto before and despite their being firm friends, Magneto has since taken a more dubious path which Xavier cannot condone. Now it seems that Magneto is about to launch a barrage of missiles with no regard for human life... only the X-MEN can stop him.

4. DEADLY REUNIONS
Written by Donald Glut
FTD: 23rd January 1993

Sabretooth is being treated at the mansion, despite Wolverine's objections, but the major threat is still Magneto, who faces the X-MEN again, this time questioning the absence of his old friend Charles Xavier. Storm is injured and her claustrophobia becomes evident.

Finally Xavier and Magneto must face each other. Xavier makes him relive the tragedies of his past. Meanwhile, at the mansion, Sabretooth reveals his true colours...

5. CAPTIVE HEARTS
Written by Robert N Skir & Marty Isenberg
FTD: 30th January 1993

Wolverine is slowly recovering from his encounter with Sabretooth, but is still feeling the effects. Jean helps him and both are aware of the attraction between them, but Jean loves Scott. That evening Jean and Scott go out for a meal but are captured by the Morlocks, a group of mutants living under the streets of New York. As the X-MEN race to the rescue, Callisto, the Morlock leader, holds high a limp and seemingly lifeless Cyclops. Storm challenges Callisto to a leadership battle.

6. COLD VENGEANCE
Written by Michael Edens
FTD: 6th February 1993

Wolverine has left the X-MEN's mansion and is in the Arctic. However he is not alone. Sabretooth watches from one of the ice-hills, detonating an explosion that leaves Wolverine adrift. Suffering from exposure, he is eventually found by an Inuit tribe.

Meanwhile, Gambit has heard rumours about the 'ideal' country of Genosha, where mutants and humans seem to be living in peace. Gambit, Storm and Jubilee set off on a trip to see for themselves... only to be captured.

7. SLAVE ISLAND
Written by Mark Edward Edens
FTD: 13th February 1993

Jubilee tries to escape from the cells where they are being held, but the restricting electronic collar that she is forced to wear makes getting out of the cells only a small victory. Gambit also seems to be all too willing to foil Jubilee's plans.

Gyrich and Trask discuss the Master Mold which will make more and more Sentinels, and Gambit comes face to face with a man who calls himself Cable.

The X-MEN must defeat the Master Mold as well as the Sentinels themselves if they are to win the day.

8. THE UNSTOPPABLE JUGGERNAUT
Written by Julianne Klemm
FTD: 6th March 1993

Professor Xavier is gone and much of the mansion lies in ruins. Jean tries to locate the perpetrator with the aid of Cerebro, while Wolverine sticks to more typically feral techniques.

The trail leads them to a mutant building-site worker named Colossus, but is he responsible? Meanwhile the Beast refuses another chance of a jail-break and the team must face the Juggernaut.

Note: This episode was actually screened out of order on its first run. Its listing here is placed in the correct running order.

9. THE CURE
Written by Mark Edward Edens
FTD: 20th February 1993

Cable attacks the Alpine home of Warren Worthington III, looking for a scientist.

Dr Gottfried Adler is renting space on Muir Island from Xavier's old friend Moira MacTaggert. Charles and Moira believe that Adler may have found a 'cure' for mutations and the X-MEN have different opinions on what the implications of such a treatment could be; for Rogue it could be an answer to her prayers.

However Adler is not the person he/she appears to be and other, more Apocalyptic forces are pulling the strings!

BIOGRAPHY

1st Appearance: INCREDIBLE HULK #180

WOLVERINE

Of all the X-MEN, Wolverine is, perhaps, the most mysterious. He has few memories that he can be sure are truly real. Before he joined the X-Men he worked for the Canadian Secret Service and has kept in contact with the now defunct super-group Alpha Flight. He has also served as a freelance intelligence operative. Logan (no other name known) has discovered that many of the memories he had were, in fact, implants. It seems that at one time he belonged to a covert unit that also included Sabretooth and Maverick. For years he possessed bones that were laced with adamantium, an unbreakable metal alloy. This bonding process was the work of a sinister figure known as 'The Professor', whose motives remain a mystery. Combined with his own natural healing factor, the 'claws' or blades that are mounted in his forearms (unsheathed through his hands) and his knowledge of martial art fighting techniques, these enabled Logan to be virtually indestructible. His healing factor also affects ageing, so it is impossible to be certain of his exact age.

For years, Logan has fought against his berserker instincts, knowing that sometimes they can be his only means of survival, yet deadly for those around him. He has the heart of a poet and the mind of a warrior.

Instead of striking at him, some enemies have struck out at Wolverine's team-mates and loved ones. His Japanese love, Mariko Yashida, was killed defending her clan and business interests. Her death broke his heart.

Over the months and years, his healing factor has been stretched and stretched to its limits. There have been few quiet moments for the Canadian to recharge his natural batteries. When Wolverine fought alongside the X-MEN, X-FACTOR and X-FORCE against Magneto at the funeral of Illyana Rasputin, the Master of Magnetism stripped the adamantium from Logan's body. His healing factor overloaded and it was only the determination to save his fellow X-MEN that kept him from the jaws of death. He discovered during his convalescence that the 'claws' he possessed were in fact only coated in adamantium. He had been born with them.

Feeling that he was a liability to the team, he left the X-MEN to begin a new chapter in his life, trying to discover some of the real truths behind his shadowy, distorted past.

10 COME THE APOCALYPSE
Written by Michael Edens
FTD: 27th February 1993

It seems as if 'Dr Adler' has indeed kept his promise to Warren Worthington when the millionaire appears minus his wings. There is no shortage of further candidates for the treatment... and soon Apocalypse has assembled his deadly Horsemen of the Apocalypse.

The X-MEN are alerted to his attack on a World Peace Conference and Rogue seeks to get as much information from Mystique as she can. She learns the truth about the so-called cure, but it may be up to Archangel to save the day!

11 DAYS OF FUTURE PAST – PART ONE
Written by Julia Jane Lewald
FTD: 13th March 1993

New York... the year 2055. Wolverine and Forge are attempting to send the feral X-Man back in time and prevent an assassination that triggers a dark and violent future history. Before they are ready, the Sentinels attack and Bishop is forced on the perilous journey in Wolverine's place.

The trip down-time leaves Bishop drained and confused, but he does remember two vitally important things: that he must stop the killing of a senior politician, and that the assassin is destined to be one of the X-MEN!

12 DAYS OF FUTURE PAST – PART TWO
Written by Robert N. Skir & Marty Isenberg
FTD: 20th March 1993

Bishop, Wolverine and Gambit remain at the mansion, while the rest of the team travel to Washington D.C. to find the location of the future assassination.

Gambit escapes and heads for Washington with Bishop and Wolverine in hot pursuit. It looks as if Bishop was correct as Gambit stands over Senator Kelly and has to be prevented from killing the anti-mutant politician.

13 THE FINAL DECISION
Written by Mark Edward Edens
FTD: 27th March 1993

Across the United States, anti-mutant crowds gather as word of Senator Kelly's kidnapping spreads. With watches stopping around the kidnap site, only one man can be behind the crime, Magneto.

But even Magneto has not counted on a new threat from an old enemy and the rescue of the Senator is the prelude to an even greater threat as Bolivar Trask's creations look to the words of a new master.

Only the X-MEN can save the Senator, but this time the odds against them are overwhelming...

Wolverine and Morph.

SEASON 2

14 'TIL DEATH DO US PART – PART ONE
Written by Mark Edward Edens
FTD: 23rd October 1993

The Beast returns to the Mansion with a full Presidential Pardon, just in time to catch the wedding bouquet of the new Mr and Mrs Summers. Finally, Jean and Scott have tied the knot, but not everyone is quite as ecstatic as the happy couple.

Wolverine is working off his aggression in the Danger Room and the new President Kelly is facing opposition to his new moderate policy on mutants.

There's further worry at the Mansion when the members of the X-MEN seem to be acting oddly and Xavier gets a message from Magneto...

15 'TIL DEATH DO US PART – PART TWO
Written by Mark Edward Edens
FTD: 30th October 1993

Away from the mansion, Jean and Scott are enjoying their honeymoon... but a sinister force seems intent on bringing their voyage to a sudden conclusion.

Storm is hospitalised after her run in with a violent mob as the rest of the X-MEN begin to realise that there are some strange claims being made by each member that contradict the others' versions.

Xavier believes that they are under attack by some mind-altering device, but Wolverine's senses tell him that the threat is a lot closer than they might think.

Meanwhile in Antarctica, Xavier and Magneto come face to face for perhaps the final time...

NOTE: In all of the following episodes a continuous sub-plot runs through each episode. This is the 'Savage Land Progression' and tells the story of Xavier and Magneto's battle to stay alive in the ancient jungle under the snowy peaks of Antarctica.

16 WHATEVER IT TAKES
Written by Julia Jane Lewald
FTD: 6th November 1993

Jean and Beast have been trying to locate the Professor using Cerebro, but are now monitoring a strange reading from Africa just as Storm returns from hospital. The location of this tear in the astral plane is Mount Kilimanjaro, Storm's old home and a young African mutant named Mjnari is all too aware of the condition.

The Shadow King is trying to return to the physical plane and thinks nothing of possessing any available human vessel to do so. Storm and the X-MEN must fight one of the missing Xavier's oldest foes, but in the end success or failure is very much in the arms of Mjnari as he tries to save the woman he calls 'Mother'.

Meanwhile Wolverine is trying to track Morph, who, in turn, is facing a battle within himself. In the Savage Land, Xavier and Magneto find they will have to work together to survive.

17 RED DAWN
Written by Ted Pedergen & Francis Moss
FTD: 13th November 1993

In the land that was once the Soviet Union, an old experiment is resumed and a long-abandoned weapon is unleashed as forces conspire to re-create old dictatorships.

In America, with the Friends of Humanity causing more trouble, it seems that nowhere is safe, even for Jubilee, who has been left behind – again. Luckily for her, when trouble comes knocking she has some assistance from Colossus.

Jubilee leaves a note for the X-MEN to find. It reads: 'Gone to Black Sea with Colossus to stop some guy named Omega Red. Dinner's in the freezer. Have a nice day...'

As Wolverine realises all too soon... Jubilee is going to find herself waaaaay out of her league!

18 REPO MAN
Written by Len Wein
FTD: 20th November 1993

Before Wolverine joined the X-MEN, he was a member of the Canadian super-group, the government-sponsored ALPHA FLIGHT. It seems that he didn't get anybody's permission to leave and now, with the money they invested in him, the Canadian government wants him back... and they're using ALPHA FLIGHT to bring him whether he likes it or not.

It's old team-mates against each other in a battle that revives many painful memories for Wolverine, including the experiment that originally produced Wolverine as Weapon X.(Len Wein, creator of the 'new' second-generation UNCANNY X-MEN, wrote the plot and script for this episode, which encompasses a great deal of Wolverine's early history in Marvel Comics' 'Weapon X' series in MARVEL COMICS PRESENTS and flashbacks in ALPHA FLIGHT. Len Wein also contributed the first part of the 'Rebirth' story at the end of the second season.)

19 X-TERNALLY YOURS
Written by Julianne Klemm
FTD: 4th December 1993

A training session in the Danger Room proves a little too much for Cyclops when Gambit is distracted mid-program by a phone call from the past. A promise and a debt of honour must be paid or Gambit's brother will die as part of an ancient pact by the Guild of Thieves.

But it seems that some promises are made to be broken, as Gambit and Belladonna are destined to discover when members of the X-MEN are forced to play their own aces.

20. TIME FUGITIVES – PART ONE
Written by Michael Edens
FTD: 11th December 1993

It's 3999 A.D. and a temporal disruption alerts Cable that the past has been dangerously altered. The cause of this time-distortion is a man from the 21st century called Bishop.

In the 21st century, Bishop arrives home fresh from saving the life of Senator Kelly, but something is wrong. Forge informs him that a plague has fallen across the world and no one has heard of the X-MEN. Bishop must return to the 20th century to secure the future, but Cable's future depends on Bishop's failure. Whose future must be saved?

21. TIME FUGITIVES – PART TWO
Written by Elliot Maggin
FTD: 18th December 1993

Fear is spreading across the world, linking the newest instances of the plague with mutants. Henry McCoy, the Beast, tries to assure everyone that there is proof that the infection is manmade. Meanwhile, the Friends of Humanity and its leader Graydon Creed fan the flames of fear.

Cable has returned to the 20th century and must alter the flow of recent events, knowing full well that in doing so he is securing a series of events that ensure that both he and Apocalypse live on. But Bishop is equally committed to his own future.

22. I REMEMBER MAMA
Written by Marty Isenberg & Robert N. Skir
FTD: 8th January 1994

With the Professor still missing, Rogue finally has to admit that he was helping her with certain 'past' problems. Since the treatments ceased she has been experiencing 'flashes'. The most recent of these involved a familiar face in the crowd, a woman who seems to have a connection with a lightning-styled insignia. So why can't Rogue remember who the woman is?

Suddenly Rogue feels a new presence in her mind – a ghost from the past who will no longer be silenced.

In a hospital a woman sleeps, tended by two nurses. She is referred to as Jane Doe, and seems to be in a deep coma. Her real name is Carol Danvers and she has every reason to hate Rogue.

23. BEAUTY AND THE BEAST
Written by Stephanie J. Mathison
FTD: 15th January 1994

The Beast is a consulting physician on the case of a young blind girl named Carly. He is all ready to assist in the operation to restore her sight, when her angry father demands that no mutant must touch his daughter.

The Friends of Humanity continue their campaign and think nothing of attacking the hospital where Carly is being treated. To them, someone who associates with mutants is almost as bad as a mutant. But they have reckoned without Beast finding his fiercer side and Wolverine proving that his subtlety is as good as his fighting.

24. MOJOVISION
Written by Brooks Wachtel
FTD: 19th January 1994

Who says there's nothing good on television any more? In a distant dimension, the crazed ratings-magus MOJO is trying to decide on a new hit show. It has to be action-filled; it has to be thrilling; it has to be THE X-MEN!

Shopping for a new television (thanks to Jubilee's latest 'accident') Scott and Jean come face to screen with the crazed alien programmer who wants to sign them up to an exclusive contract. The problem is that television executives take rejection very badly and psychotic, spineless, alien television executives don't take rejection at all. Action.

25. BIRTH AND REBIRTH – PART ONE
Written by Len Wein
FTD: 5th February 1994

Xavier and Magneto are battling for their lives in the Savage Land as pieces of a carefully formulated plan begin to fall into place. Even their sudden rescuer Ka-Zar is but a pawn in a much bigger game.

Mr Sinister has forced Morph to summon the X-MEN to Australia and in turn Morph tries to warn them of his forced betrayal. Scott and Jean learn of Sinister's plans, but even if they are flying into a trap, can they turn down their only chance of finding the Professor?

26. BIRTH AND REBIRTH – PART TWO
Written by Michael Edens
FTD: 12th February 1994

Sinister has the X-MEN imprisoned in the citadel and announces his intentions, particularly his plans for Jean, Scott and Magneto.

Wolverine and Ka-Zar discover they have a common enemy and launch a last-ditch mission to rescue the X-MEN and Ka-Zar's wife Shanna. But the X-MEN are without their powers and with Mr Sinister's plans nearing completion, the odds are not in the mutants' favour. To succeed even past enemies will have to work together and new alliances will be forged.

AND FI

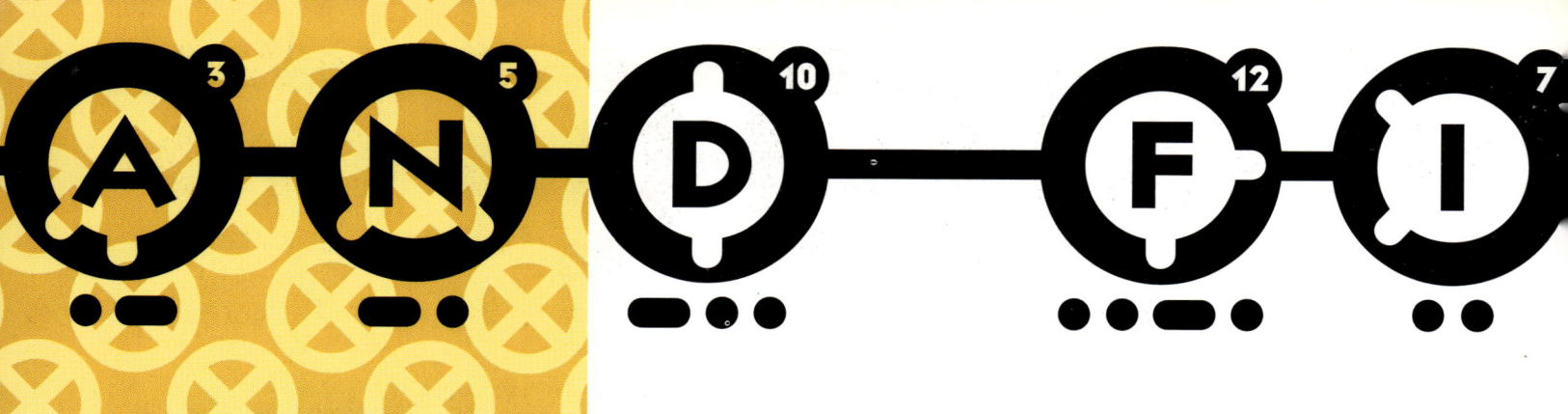

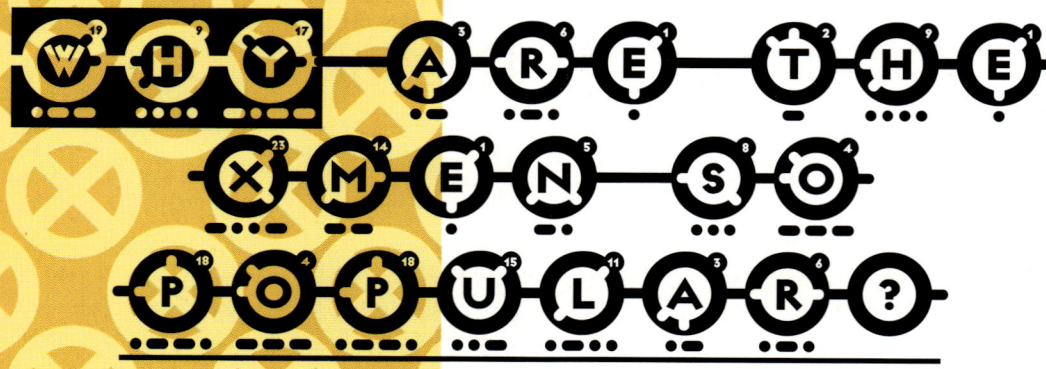

WHY ARE THE X-MEN SO POPULAR?

In fact, why are all comics (and their grown-up cousins the 'graphic novels') more popular than ever?

It's a little like asking why a particular song means so much to one person and nothing to another. In short, a definitive answer is probably impossible to put down on paper. For different people the X-MEN are different things, though it may be possible to find some common ground.

NALLY

Paranoia?

THE X-MEN.

I'D NEVER SEEN THEM BEFORE, BUT I'D HEARD OF THEM.

SUPER-POWERED MUTANTS. FREAKS. THEY LOOKED JUST LIKE NORMAL PEOPLE --

-- BUT YOU NEVER COULD TELL.

STAY BACK! DON'T TOUCH ME!

YOU HEARD THE LADY! BACK OFF!

WHAT'SA MATTER, GIRLIE? REAL HUMANS NOT GOOD ENOUGH FOR YA?

SAME TO YOU!

WE DON'T WANT YOUR KIND AROUND HERE!

THEY WERE CRIMINALS -- KILLERS --

STINKIN' MUTIES!

WE MOVED IN --

And Finally

There are times in every person's life when he or she feels alone, out of place, unimportant or just plain bored. Life can be, at times, a very mundane place to live, and comics provide a ray of light, a brief interlude that gives us a chance to escape the grey world for a much more colourful universe.

Few of us can project eye-beams, control the weather or have unbreakable claws we can unleash (though there are times when we wish we could), but through comics we can identify with those who do have these extraordinary talents

'The X-MEN give readers an escape from ordinary life,' says Bob Harras, Editor of the X-Titles. 'They can do things we can't but at the same time they have problems we can relate to.'

But there's more to it all than wish fulfilment. Comics are, more and more, appealing to people of all ages in a world that forces children to grow up all too quickly. Perhaps quite rightly comics have to be careful what they portray and how. Characters in comics can no longer be seen in 'black and white' terms. Good and Evil are less clearly defined and much harder to recognise.

The X-MEN, perhaps more than most comics, show us the problems that people face as individuals and as families. They aren't always away saving the universe. More often than not, they are trying to come to terms with who and what they are, trying to expand their talents and finding their place in the sometimes unfriendly world. They don't always win; they don't even get on with each other all the time. In fact some members, as in life, distrust and dislike one another. All, whether they care to admit it or not, have their own agendas within this 'family', all too aware of the strings that bind them and divide them. All have made decisions they have regretted and choices that have seen them through.

The word 'heroes' is often bandied about in less than appropriate ways. But the X-MEN are good examples. They stand up for what they believe to be right, no matter what that cost may be. It's a lot harder to fight for someone who doesn't want your help than it is to 'go to bat' for someone who does, being all too aware that if that situation was reversed, there might be no one there for you.

Tim Quinn, head of Marvel UK's 'Special Projects', believes that the team was special from the beginning. 'Stan Lee and Jack Kirby created characters we could believe in. From the start, here was a group of characters who had great adventures, but the stories were more than that. Stan's whole concept was ingenious. The team may have been through lots of changes, but I think the reason the comics are such a success is because the basic idea — of people learning about themselves and the way they relate to people — is still there and people can identify with that. The X-MEN may always be the underdogs, but they never give in.'

The X-MEN are forever human. Even as mutants, they strive against the odds to do the best they can. It's a feeling we can all identify with to some degree. For mutant read deviant. For the Legacy Virus, read cancer or AIDS. Remove the labels and the Marvel Universe suddenly seems a lot closer to our own.

'You have to remember that back in 1963, the year the comic first appeared, America was going through some pretty rough times. Kennedy would be assassinated before the second issue came out and America was fighting controversial enemies. The X-MEN represent some of the paranoia that the country had been feeling in the wake of the McCarthy hearings,' explains Steve Holland, editor of COMIC WORLD. 'The X-MEN were seen as the "enemy" by "normal" people, judged guilty for being different. The X-MEN argued for tolerance and proper understanding.'

But it's not blind faith the X-MEN operate on. Like any dream or ideal, it is something that can and should be questioned and made stronger because of it. There have been casualties in reaching for that dream. Few things mean more than those which are difficult to achieve and most faiths agree that it's the travelling that is more important than the destination.

They are two dimensional illustrations brought to life by skilful art and thought-provoking words. There have been classic stories. The best ones are those in which we can identify with a character or situation, recognising a decision or event in our own lives. Through the pages of the X-MEN, we see those characters make their choices. Sometimes it's the right one, on other occasions it's not. It's a little like life, but the comic allows us to view it from a safer distance.

'That's what Marvel tries to do. We take great pride in telling great stories,' says Bob Harras.

Marvel's Editor-in Chief, Tom DeFalco agrees: 'Marvel produces many comic books every month. The best stories are classics, the ones that mean something, that strike a chord... and the worst? The worst comic story from Marvel at any given time is still a good read, so everyone's happy!'

If at worst the adventures of the X-MEN are still a good read, a soap opera in comic form, at best it's a whole new world — but one very like our own — to explore, enjoy and learn from. In the end you can't fight bigotry and prejudice with guns, fists or convenient super-powers. Ultimately, it's simply down to words and the willingness to back those words with everything you've got. That what makes the X-MEN different and that's what makes them make a difference. That what makes anyone — in the Marvel Universe or the world outside your own door — a real hero.

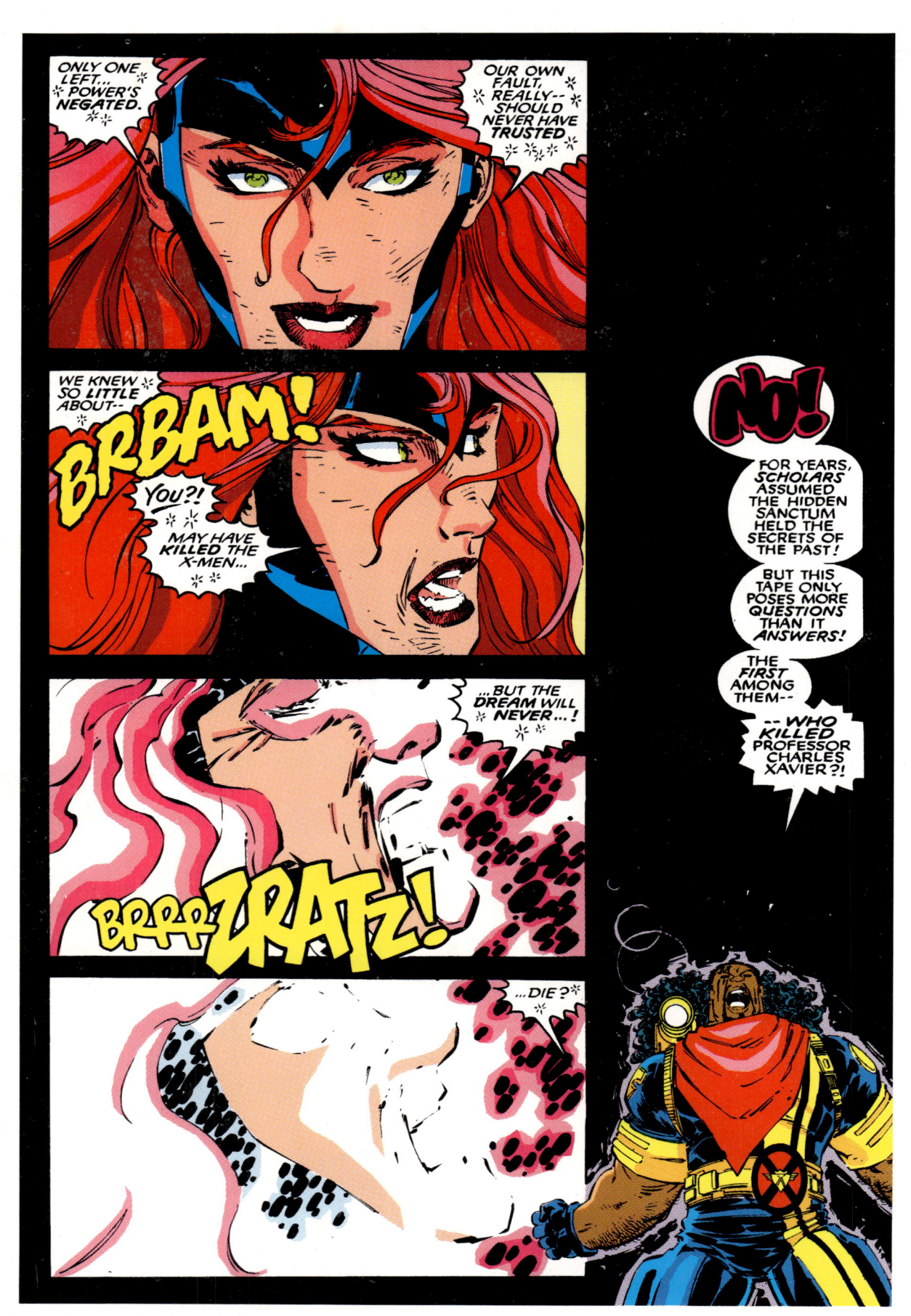

What does the future hold?